The Post-War English Novel

A Study in Humanism

The Post-War English Novel

A Study in Humanism

Rudra Prasad Mahto

PRESTIGE

PRESTIGE BOOKS
3/28, East Patel Nagar
New Delhi 110 008

ISBN: 81-7551-112-5

Printed at Chaman Offset Press, New Delhi 110 002

CONTENTS

Acknowledgements

First of all I express my gratitude to Dr. K.K. Sinha, Principal, S.S. Memorial College, Ranchi, for his insightful suggestions, encouragement and help which enabled me to complete this book.

I owe my gratitude to Professor D.D. Baskiyar, former head of the English Department, Ranchi University, Ranchi who helped me in many ways in completing this book.

I am really fortunate to receive encouragement and help from the retired Principal of my college, Dr. N.K. Singh, he deserves my thanks. I also appreciate the cooperation extended by my colleagues. I am thankful to my friend Professor G. Mehta, Department of English, Marwari College, Ranchi.

I must thank the librarians and other members of the staff of the National Library, Calcutta, and the CIEFL Library, Hyderabad, for their help.

I am highly obliged to Dr. Panchanan Mahto who not only gave me brotherly affection but also encouraged me both in academic and non-academic matters.

My wife Sumitra Suman has always been a source of inspiration for me; her shouldering of the responsibility to look after the family provided me with sufficient time to carry on this project smoothly. While I was writing this book, the sweet smile of my daughters Namrata, Amrita, Vinita and Shweta gave me fresh energy to complete my work.

Rudra Prasad Mahto

Chapter I

INTRODUCTION

Humanism is a philosophy—the central concern of which is man and his happiness. It underlies the value and dignity of man and takes him as the measure of all things. All knowledge as well as human institutions are deemed useful only when they help man realize his potentialities. Generally Western and Eastern philosophers hold that what matters for man really is this earthly existence and not the unseen other world. Therefore, man's attention should be centred on here and now as against Heaven or Hell. This also implies the rejection of supernatural and denial of a personal God. However, even those who are religious humanists firmly believe that man's ultimate concern is man himself. Humanists like Socrates, Mahatma Gandhi and Rabindra Nath Tagore have the same feeling. The quintessence of Socrates's thought lay in his firm faith in human personality as the fundamental reality whereas all social and political institutions were at best aids to human development. Virtue, knowledge and human happiness were all identical to him. Right knowledge should lead man to right action and right action to "unsullied happiness."[1] Therefore, Socrates pleaded for the acquisition of the knowledge of one's self. Thus his axiom "know thyself" forms an important tenet of humanism.

Mahatma Gandhi and Rabindra Nath Tagore also express similar views. They saw God in man and so proclaimed that the worship of God lays essentially in the service of mankind. Humanism of both has a mystical and religious bias. It would be appropriate to quote V.S. Naravane in this context:

> The ideas of both Gandhi and Tagore are rooted in those broad intellectual movements, which shaped the course of

> Indian thought in the nineteenth century. They were both humanists. Gandhi's humanism had a moral social bias while Tagore's was coloured by his aesthetic-mystical experience, but both were firm believers in the worth and dignity of the human individual. They were both to the theistic rather than the pantheistic or absolute traditions in Indian philosophy. . . . In the worldview of both Gandhi and Tagore the idea of love plays a dominant part. They regard love as the magic wand which dissolves all contraries and opens the gateway of truth.[2]

Humanism is an ancient tradition in thought. It has its own historical development like all ancient traditions. It may be said to have begun its career with the Greek philosopher Protagoras in the fifth century B.C. His famous dictum 'man is the measure of all things' is often expressed as a terse statement of the quintessence of all humanism. In due course, various doctrines on the nature of man have come into being and corresponding to each of these doctrines, various schools of humanism have arisen. It is also associated with the new learning that blossomed over Europe in the fifteenth century Renaissance. It had its roots in the discovery and dissemination of the original texts of the Greek writers. It presented the classical writers for the first time as direct commentators on life. There is also the well-known Christian humanism of the seventeenth century. What is described as Christian humanism is best represented by Erasmus. His philosophy of Christ is essentially an attempt at turning away from scientific questions to the problems of moral life and religious imagination. He insisted on "the dignity of man"[3] and argued that man was important through Christ's atonement and God's grace. He emphasized the necessity and importance of cultivating a life of integrity and pleaded for an understanding and practise of true Christianity.

Jean-Paul Sartre wants us to believe that his Existentialism is a brand of humanism. The only element recognizable as humanistic in his philosophy seems to be his daring rejection of the supernatural.

Then there is a particular variety of humanism called the Neo-Humanism. Paul Elmer More and Irving Babbitt who sought to replace both the extremes of the religious and the romantic views of life lead this Neo-Humanism. Its chief doctrine is "inner check"[4] and its chief values are harmony and restraint: "After all to be a good humanist is merely to be moderate and sensible and decent."[5]

The principal aim of the Neo-humanists is to create a synthesis for all that is good in ancient cultures and religions after rejecting the belief in a transcendental deity.

The relationship between a humanist and a novelist is very close; or in other words the humanist and the novelist are intimate ones and the association between the two "is not accidental."[6] Humanism has often found expression in the novel. D.H. Lawrence argued this in his vigorous essay "Morality and the Novel" (1925) for the value of his chosen form by asserting its moral function:

> Philosophy, religion, science, they are all of them busy nailing things down to get a stable equilibrium. Religion with its nailed-down One God, who says Thou Shalt, Thou shan't and hammers home every time; philosophy, with its fixed ideas; science with its 'laws'; they all of them, all of the time want to nail us on some tree or other.
>
> But the novel, no. The novel is the highest example of subtle inter-relatedness that man has discovered. Everything is true in its own time, place and circumstance. If you try to nail anything down in the novel, either it kills the novel, or the novel gets up and runs away with the nail.[7]

D.H. Lawrence places the novel at the centre of humanistic culture because of its unique closeness to human experience.

George Eliot also expresses similar views. She is always concerned with the problems of human personality and its relationship with forces outside itself. Her *Middlemarch* (1871-72) is a remarkable novel and is important "for its noble humanism and the criticism of life and the arts . . . during the years of the Industrial Revolution."[8]

Henry James also makes it clear that his "central concern is with human beings."[9] He is the most undoctrinaire writer; and he was praised by T.S. Eliot because "he has a mind so fine that no idea could violate it." *The Portrait of a Lady* (1881) is considered to be the masterpiece of his early period. Its heroine Isabel Archer shows James working in the tradition of George Eliot and through her he expresses the centrality of his concern for human freedom and his fear of those forces institutionalized in the Church or simply embodied in egocentric human beings which threaten that freedom.

F.R. Leavis in his essay on E.M. Forster in *The Common Pursuit* (1952) describes *A Passage to India* (1924) as "a classic of the liberal spirit." E.M. Forster in *A Passage to India* gives a searching and convincing account, of one attempt to make liberal-humanist values work under difficult circumstances. Speaking of E.M. Forster's humanism, Fredrick C. Crews says: "Forster's whole position as a humanist or as a man, who places his faith in this world and he takes the individual, human norm as the measure of everything."[11]

E.M. Forster provides ideal resolutions for many of the conflicts explored in the novels. For him, the great happiness is to build little islands of safety. The islands of personal relationships can be reached only by a few rare souls. The moments of insight between Margaret and Helen in *Howards End* (1910) are the exceptions in the present day society.

The connection between humanism and fiction is an old and intimate one. Commenting on the essential relationship between novel and humanism Robert Liddel says: "the novelist ought to be a humanist. And since the novel itself is not a thing that has ever been very precisely defined it is clearly improbable that any very precise terms can with propriety be applied to the novelist."[12]

Whatever it may be, the novelist's function has always been to know human nature and to convey to the mankind in fictional terms the most thorough knowledge of human nature and the happiest delineation of its varieties. If a novelist has to know human nature thoroughly and to think its varieties worth delineating, then his values must be fundamentally humanist values. Thus it is the writer's duty to help man by lifting his heart by encouraging him and by making him aware of hope, honour and pride which have been the glory of human beings.

But in the present day, it is difficult to make a humanistic affirmation that does not simplify itself into political rhetoric. Virginia Woolf's husband Leonard Woolf describes the atmosphere of the 1930s in the following manner:

> I have reached the period in my autobiography in which our lives and the lives of everyone have become penetrated, dominated by politics. Happy the country and era—if there can ever have been one—which has no politics. Ever since 1914 in the background of our living and thoughts have loomed the menace of politics, the canker of public events.[13]

The period was not distinguished for its novels, perhaps for this reason, though Evelyn Waugh and previously Graham Greene were writing successfully from a Catholic point of view. But in George Orwell a major humanistic writer did emerge.

Although Orwell may be thought of as a writer of the 1930s because of his social concern, he regards Communism as a panacea than Catholicism. In *Keep the Aspidistra Flying* (1936) the central character Gordon Comstock talks to the wealthy Socialist Revolution about the perplexities of the time:

> "We're stuck the Buridan's donkey. Only there are three alternatives instead of two and all three of them make us spew. Socialism's only one of them."
>
> "And what are the other two?"
>
> "Oh, I suppose suicide and the Catholic Church."[14]

Orwell's life shows him continually trying to define an attitude to life that would help humanity out of its impasse.

In modern time it is difficult for a novelist to become a humanist. The violent changes in class structure, the breakdown of traditional beliefs and the threats of war have brought many a writer to complete abandonment of humanist belief. According to Malcolm Bradbury: "In most of the Western literature the world war of 1913-45 seems to mark a watershed; and in the novel this coincides with the emergence of a new group of writers with new problems."[15]

But the new novelists are generally concerned with the incoherence of the present day society and disintegration of men. However, it is our belief that some of the major Post-War novelists namely John Wain, Iris Murdoch, William Golding, Kingsley Amis, Doris Lessing and Angus Wilson, who deal with the transfiguration of the British class structure in the twentieth century, are essentially concerned with human values and in their novels the essential focus is always upon the consciousness of their characters who find themselves lonely in a hostile world. They are alive to the responsibility to enlighten humanity and fight against the modern despair and try to rebuild the broken fragments of optimistic humanism, being deeply involved in the restoration and reconstruction of the will. Humanism to us is a conception of life that makes man more prosperous and hence more free, reflecting upon the innate goodness of human beings.

The next chapter of the present book treats John Wain as a novelist who is not a prophet of despair. He is primarily concerned with the despair of modern man that leads him to active humanism and he is always conscious of the basic human values. The theme of humanism emerges as a dominant theme in the novels of John Wain. There runs a constant commitment to the value of the individual and the personal, a constant assertion of the dignity of the human being throughout his fiction. The statement of man's worth gives both coherence and direction to his fiction. Charles Lumley, the protagonist of his first novel entitled *Hurry on Down* (1953), belongs to middle class. He travels through contemporary Britain and earns the right to keep his job and win the expensive prize woman. Edgar Banks, the hero of *Living in the Present* (1955) is able to discover a reason for living in the world. *The Contenders* (1958), his third novel, projects the theme of personal value into a wide area of English society. In his other novels, too, John Wain demonstrates the value and the importance of the humane. His central characters find themselves in their place, and their virtues lay in enormous stress on the dignity of human, the personal and the individual value.

The third chapter is devoted to an analysis of the theme of humanism in the novels of Iris Murdoch. She is a literary artist who has a purpose that gives significance to her realistic presentation of life. Her ties to the nineteenth century tradition, so evident in the nostalgia with which she refers to the "rich receding background"[16] of reality in Victorian novels act as a welcome reminder of unfreedom. The theme of humanism is one of the most important themes of Iris Murdoch that signifies the effort of human beings to construct and particularize their own means of salvation.

Almost all the characters in the novels of Iris Murdoch seek some form of definition, some means of coherently explaining what they are. In *Under the Net* (1954), Murdoch tells the story of Jake Donaghue's wanderings about bohemian London and Paris as he attempts to find a satisfactory way of life. Imber Court, for example, the long, clean aseptic manor house in *The Bell* (1958), represents the clean and pure existence. Its inhabitants want to live in order to gain religious meaning and direction.

The fourth chapter presents William Golding as a novelist who creates innumerable forms, the truth of human suffering. He believes that the very act of creation is a form of release. An attempt is made to show William Golding's unerring concern for human beings with their future. Although Angus Wilson describes him as "an antihumanist,"[17] but we believe that he with his mind endeavours to create a paradise for human beings throughout his fictional universe. The unusual placing of his novels, for example, the Pacific island of the schoolboys in *Lord of the Flies* (1954), the Neanderthal world in *The Inheritors* (1955), the Atlantic rock in *Pincher Martin* (1956), the medieval world of *The Spire* (1964) show how far Golding is from offering the kind of realistic observation of normal society which is the central tradition of novel. His different metaphors employed in his novels can be read as orthodox and traditional Christian statements about the nature of man. Each metaphor underlies man's depravity, pride and the futility of his reason. The novels are permeated with the sense of man's sin and guilt and the images depict these qualities in conventional Christian terms.

The fifth chapter presents Kingsley Amis as a humanist who treats various human themes on several intellectual and social levels. He tries to give the expression to the difficulties, passion and strain of social condition. He is also concerned with the problems of individual human beings. In the novels of Kingsley Amis, the concept of humanism is essentially connected with "the theme of the adjustment of the individual."[18] The theme of the novels is ultimately adjustment, adjustment of the individual and his aims to the wider society in which he lives. The central characters of Amis's novels support the Labour Party and the Welfare State. Social and moral references abound because man deals with social and moral facts continuously. The hero of *Lucky Jim* (1954), Jim Dixon, is always conscious of the dignity of human beings. He is the true representative of middle class people. While he always thinks of the welfare of the people of this class, he hates the filthy rich. Heroes in later Amis's novels are able to handle themselves and their worlds more successfully. In *I Like It Here* (1958), Garnet Bowen is a freelance writer. His wife keeps insisting that the sloppy involvement is immoral and he must give up the project and assert his own convictions. In *Take a Girl Like You* (1960), morality is the subject of incessant debate but does not affect the outcome of the story and yet Amis's heroes talk a great deal about honesty and integrity.

The sixth chapter treats humanistic preoccupations of Doris Lessing. For Doris Lessing the clouds are dark but she is also aware of the silver linings. She is committed to active persuasion to reform society. She talks of the sense of duty that makes her join organization and defends her own support for Communism. Her sense of social responsibility leads her to search for her values and for her literary material among the working class in London. Her commitment to a sense of social responsibility and a pursuit of those oppressed by society also infuses her fiction about Colonial Africa and makes her theme humanistic. Her first novel *The Grass is Singing* (1950) is a remarkable novel. Her intense feeling of political and social responsibility is carefully worked into specific historical situation reflecting upon the essential human situations. In *The Golden Notebook* (1962), she tackles the two problems: differences between White and Black in Africa and the problem of women's liberation in man's society. In *The Four-Gated City* (1969), Martha with Mark and Jack finds in sex an even more expansive fusion between self and world, an access to "an impersonal current . . . the impersonal sea."[19]

In the seventh chapter, Angus Wilson's humanistic outlook on man and his life is explained. It intends to study the humanism of Angus Wilson. The important novels of Angus Wilson which deal with the theme of humanism are *Hemlock and After* (1952) and *The Old Men at the Zoo* (1961). These novels have relevance not merely to the modern situation but also to the human predicament. His novels deal with the condition of human soul which always tries to win new frontiers of consciousness. His memorable characters are generally humanists who struggle against the anti-humanist forces of the society. *The Middle Age of Mrs. Eliot* (1958), the third novel of Angus Wilson, is successful in conveying through two major characters Meg Eliot and David two forms of humanistic achievement as active and passive responses to the challenges of modern life.

The concluding chapter sums up the arguments of the present study and shows that the novelists in question are humanists and their novels are an attempt to find possible solutions to the problems and sufferings of human life caused particularly by the abnormal pressure and tension that prevail in our time.

In outlining a society full of class changes, judgements and distinctions, these contemporary writers often exhibit and express sympathy for the underdogs, for those not granted the automatic privileges of an inherited position within the Establishment. The social and political attitudes that they express are filtered through individual emotions and reactions.

NOTES

1. G.S. Balarama Gupta, *Humanism: An Overview* (Calcutta: Writers Workshop, 1983), p. 11.
2. V.S. Naravane, *Modern Indian Thought* (Bombay: Kitab Mahal, 1964), p. 113.
3. G.S. Balrama Gupta, p. 14.
4. T.S. Eliot, *Selected Essays* (London: Faber & Faber, 1951), p. 476.
5. Irving Babbitt, *Rousseau and Romanticism* (New York: Meridian Books, 1919), p. xxi.
6. Peter Faulkner, *Humanism in the English Novel* (London: Elek/Pemberton, 1975), p. 3.
7. *Loc. cit.*
8. J.N. Mundra, *The English Novel* (Bareilly: Prakash, 1969), p. 283.
9. Peter Faulkner, p. 72.
10. *Loc. cit.*
11. Fredrick C. Crews, Introduction, *E.M. Forster: The Perils of Humanism* (London: O.U.P., 1962), p. 6.
12. Robert Liddel, *A Treatise on the English Novel* (London: Jonathan Cape, 1947), pp. 53-54.
13. Peter Faulkner, *Humanism in the English Novel*, p. 133.
14. *Ibid.*, p. 146.
15. Malcolm Bradbury, *Possibilities: Essays on the State of the Novel* (London: O.U.P., 1973), p. 216.
16. Iris Murdoch, "Against Dryness," *Encounter*, XVI, Jan. 1961, p. 20.
17. Angus Wilson, "Dilemma of the Contemporary Novelist," Kerry Mesweeney, ed., *Diversity and Depth in Fiction* (London: Secker and Warburg, 1983), p. 247.
18. James Gindin, *Post-war British Fiction: New Accents and Attitudes* (London: Cambridge University Press, 1962), p. 41.
19. Doris Lessing, *The Four-Gated City* (London: McGibbon and Kee, 1969), p. 496.

Chapter II

JOHN WAIN

John Wain's awareness of the despair of modern man leads him to active humanism and he never allows basic human values to slip away from his grasp. The theme of humanism emerges as a dominant theme in the novels of John Wain. In his first three novels—*Hurry on Down* (1953), *Living in the Present* (1955) and *The Contenders* (1958)—we have the sense of "constant commitment to the value of the individual and the personal, a constant assertion of the dignity of the human being."[1] Although frequently describing and satirizing a world of chaotic folly, each of the novels contains a central statement of the "moral worth of the individual."[2] The statement of man's worth, qualified and limited as it may be, gives both coherence and direction to his fiction. Charles Lumley, the hero of Wain's first novel *Hurry on Down* belongs to the commercial middle class. He deliberately turns his back on university education and takes on jobs that are manual, menial or even illegal while trying to find and establish his own identity in society. He is protesting against the established norms and values in contemporary society. Jimmy Porter in John Osborne's *Look Back in Anger* (1956) rails against the class structure, established religion and the prevalent apathy generated by the modern world. He, too, refuses employment suitable for a university graduate in protest. It is the same spirit of rebellion against probably outdated social hierarchy. John Osborne in his play *Look Back in Anger* tackles the problem of "hypergamy,"[3] that is, the marriage of a young man with a woman above his status. Jimmy Porter, the hero of the play, is called the typical "bull in the China shop,"[4] at any rate until the belatedly emotional and optimistic scene in which the quarrelling spouses are reconciled around a plush teddy bear. Incidentally, it may have been this final drop of rose water poured into the gall and vitriol that made the pill acceptable and secured public approval. Even Kingsley Amis's Jim Dixon, the protagonist of *Lucky Jim*, finds university education and background a sham and prefers private employment. John Braine's working class hero, Joe Lampton's (*Room at the Top*, 1957) rejection of his background and his desire to climb to the top is stronger than Sillitoe's critical acceptance of the working class background and status.

In this novel John Braine shows his realistic observation, restraint and dramatic dynamism. It has also sounded a new note, in as much as the author has ceased to plead a case and is "more concerned to elucidate the complexity of human motives."[5]

Walter Allen has rightly observed that the hero of John Wain's *Hurry on Down* does not fit in one job; rather he moves from job to job in following words: "the possessor of the mediocre degree in history from Oxford and a driving obsession to avoid the phoney in life, becomes in turn a window-cleaner, a driver of motor cars for export, a dope smuggler, a hospital orderly, a chauffeur, a chucker out in a night club and a gag writer for radio shows."[6]

Even though he washes windows, he is aware how foolish it would be to regard himself as a part of the working class:

> Charles thought with a sense of self-congratulation, he had always been right about them, right to despise them for their idiotic attempt to look through two telescopes at the same time: one fashioned of German psychology and pointed at themselves, the other of Russian economics and directed at the English working class.[7]

Yet Charles can neither ignore nor resign from society. Each of his jobs is involved with society and carries some sort of class identification.

Along with his contemporary writers, John Wain turns to the traditional values of the working class. They value the working class for its responses within a society. The problems of the working class have in one sense become the problems of many of the thoughtful men in the whole society; how to assert and defend oneself in the midst of chaos and indifference.

Perhaps it is the sense of localism that makes the humanism of John Wain "more optimistic."[8] Here localism means attachment of one person to his country and to follow the culture and style of the same country instead of imitating the other culture and way of life. The longing for localism keeps a man at his best and John Wain's people are no exception to it. Gindin's words are worth quoting here: "Man is best, in Wain's fiction, when he sticks with what he knows and can handle when he avoids the pretence implicit in the cosmopolitan and the universal." (138)

This sense of localism may, however, also be seen in *Hurry on Down.* When the protagonist of the novel, Charles Lumley, goes to Rosa's house to meet the members of her family, he likes only her father with his pre-First World War habit:

> Charles liked Rosa's father . . . it was a pleasure to hear her father, whose speech had been formed along with all his other habits before 1914, the last injection of new elements into his vocabulary had been in the trenches of a slight seasoning of the Army slang of those days gave his talk a touch of colour. (175)

But Charles Lumley does not feel any sense of respect for Stan, Rosa's younger brother. In him he finds a dearth of local colour. He slurs his speech and prides himself on "his commercial success and his American cigarettes."[9] It is his imitation of the west that keeps aloof from localism Charles is fond of:

> He did not like Stan. At sixty Stan would have neither the massive good humour nor the genuine dignity of his father . . . it was demonic English of mid-twentieth century rapid slurred, essentially a city dialect and, in origin, essentially American. (115)

Localism is also found in John Wain's *The Contenders.* The hero, Joe Shaw, develops in a way that Wain thinks "natural and good."[10] He is unconcerned with the "struggle for power."[11] Instead he prefers looking for a lady "who has developed untouched by modern commercial society."[12] In other words, the spirit of localism is in him and he wants to see it in his better half as well. He is convinced that a true growth of personality is possible: "Everyone's life has same shape, the shape it would grow into if it was left alone, like a tree. Most people tinker about with the shape and distort it more or less either because they want to."[13]

John Wain's novels do represent life. He knows "the best that the novel can do . . . is not to offer a refuge from actual life."[14] His characters hold the mirror to the intelligent middle class and his mature customer finds himself within the arena of his judgement. A discerning humanism and a quality of imaginative realism mark the stuff of all his novels. He has been successful in feeling the pulse of contemporary society and its people.

Significantly, John Wain is always interested in saying something about the people first and foremost. All the same, he never forgets to tell about the lives of people in society. The theme of his novels is profoundly rooted in the study of man in society. His is a world where common men of the contemporary society exist. He knows that he cannot write a novel if he has "the illusion that only a special kind of world is worth writing about."[15] Thus, the novels of John Wain, when judged by the yard-stick of Henry James, remain a "direct impression of life and they do represent life."

Besides, while letting his novel function as a mirror of the contemporary life, John Wain has perhaps tried his utmost to preserve human dignity. This preservation of human dignity may be seen right from *Hurry on Down* to *A Winter in the Hills.* As Wain has seen and felt the devaluation of human stature after the Second World War, he has a strong sense of the basic need that human dignity has to be preserved. This can be seen clearly in Edgar Banks's attempt in *Living in the Present* to "preserve life."[16] The key phrase death destroys men itself substantiates John Wain's keen desire to maintain human dignity. In the later novels, the theme of the preservation of human dignity is deepened and applied to wider areas of individual and social experience. Wain's defences of the individual's dignity have become deeper, more central to the contemporary world and above all less vitiated by sentimentality or self-pity.

In his other novels John Wain, too, demonstrates the value and importance of the humane. His heroes find themselves in their place, and their virtues lay enormous stress on the "dignity of humane,"[17] the personal and the individual value.

But the people were feeling the hangover of the war in the period of John Wain. All people—whether soldiers or civilians—suffered in varying intensities. They were far from happy and felt insecure. Human dignity was at stake. This sense of insecurity and suffering had a damaging effect on culture as well, as Jack Lindsay comes to find it: "We are in the midst of a cultural crisis of which the crisis in literature is one aspect."[18]

All these agonising sense of suffering and cultural crisis relates to an understanding of the inevitable effect on a novelist's outlook. When all had suffered or were suffering, it was too much to expect of a novelist to feel compassion and sympathy for a character whose sufferings could not be more than those of the common people. Perhaps this may have led to the belief among some critics of the day that a "great new" novel had not been created since the war. In this context, Arnold Kettle remarks: "the last twenty-five years have produced as far as one can see at this close distance no great new English novels nor indeed more than a handful of books which one feels inclined to use the word good . . . it seems more likely that this will come to be seen by literary historians as a barren period . . . of sociological curiosities rather than as living art."[19]

Obviously the reputation of John Wain, belonging to this "barren" period appears to be faced with vicissitudes. In fact, critics have made many a vitriolic attack on the heroes of Wain's novels calling them anti-heroes devoid of genuine anger.

Kenneth Allosp alleges that it was "the perfect day" for John Wain's heroes to be angry and there were many things before them to be angry about, but he adds: "it is difficult to see any."[20] Fredrick R. Karl, too, makes a categorical remark that heroes of John Wain and his contemporaries do not have anger:

> Primarily, the protagonists of these novelists are not really angry. They are, however, disgruntled with themselves, with their social status, with their work, with their colleagues, with the shabbiness of daily life, with their frustrated aspirations for self-fulfilment, with the competitive spirit, with the inaccessibility of women and drink, with all the small activities whose pursuit takes up their depleted energies. If we want genuine anger we must turn to the continual novel.[21]

John Wain, like Sartre and Saul Bellow, makes a sincere attempt to exhibit human values. He also tries his utmost to indicate that it is often difficult to "understand and explain"[22] the human personality. John Wain, a defender of human dignity against writers of alienation and the void, has created in *The Smaller Sky* (1967) a novel so close in form and spirit to the classical novel of alienation *Nausea* (1938) of Jean Paul Sartre. The similarities are so glaring that it seems almost certain that Wain in 1967 was consciously drawing on Sartre's 1938 novel. The heroes of both novels are isolates. Roquentin has occasional sexual intercourse with Francoise, the café owner, Geary; the hero of *The Smaller Sky* is married to Elizabeth, but we do not hear of these relationships. The happiness of conjugal life is missing in the lives of these heroes.

Geary's worthiness of pity is in itself rewarding, whether or not he is actually pitied. He looks like the typical heroes of Saul Bellow, viz. Augie of *Augie March* (1953). Geary like Augie cannot accept success. Geary may be like Augie rejecting high positions. As Augie is "unable to accept"[23] the love of Thea or to stay with Sophie, so is Geary at Paddington Station away from his wife and son. One is reminded of the hero of Saul Bellow's *Herzog* (1964), running from the sisters, "not able to stand kindness at this time."[24]

Thus there is a closer similarity than meets the eye between Saul Bellow's "overtly masochistic heroes"[25] and Geary. The latter is therefore, not typical of fifties. John Wain produces enough "drumming sound"[26] now and then to give impetus and sometimes to mark alienation, self-hatred and masochism.

Joe Shaw, the hero of *The Contenders*, for all his home-grown perception, is often perplexed by what he notices in the people around him and at several points abandons futile attempts with others or with himself.

Like *Hurry on Down* and *Living in the Present*, *The Contenders* too ends with the protagonist finding himself and his place. Like the protagonists of the two novels, Joe Shaw, too, gets the girl as a prize, in such a way the ending sounds seem a bit sentimental. In this connection, one may quote James Gindin: "the equation between value and reward seems a little too pat and soft. Yet the value, the moral centre of Wain's work, is in its insistence on the dignity of the human and the personal, a sentimental value. In a world where a man has little understanding and less control he can at least make personal choices and at least recognize what and where he is. This is essentially a sentimental doctrine because the choices and the recognition are endowed with more emotion than they structurally or logically warrant." (143)

John Wain finds a human being full of complex and reverberating emotion and, owing to this, he is bound to be sentimental. Small wonder, the happy romance at the conclusion looks unjustifiable gesture. Indeed it is a pity Wain has not been quite successful in avoiding sentimentality. His comic devices remain too brittle, too decorative and too occasional to prevent the weight of the emotion. Perhaps he should have gone for a richer and more violent comic effect of the kind we get in Evelyn Waugh. But the comic effects achieved by John Wain are much too simple and mild.

John Wain projects the theme of personal value into a wider area of English society in his third novel *The Contenders.* A narrator, rumpled, fat, easygoing, Joe Shaw tells the story of his two schoolmates, Robert Lamb, the artist and Ned Roper, the businessman and their rise to prominence in post World War II England. Each struggles to achieve more than the other. Yet both depend on the soundness and the simplicity of Joe Shaw, who still works on the newspaper in the grubby pottery town all three of the characters came from. Although Wain ridicules both complete subservience to art as a kind of mystical goodness and the reverence for material success so prevalent in society, neither art nor business in itself is his principal target. Rather, he attacks the spirit of competition that motivates both the artist and the businessman, a spirit instilled by parents, teachers, all of society. And the hero, Joe Shaw, is simply the man in whose clouded chemistry the injection of competition did not happen to take. Competition, the desire to excel, leads to a kind of involuted egotism and represents the slavish and unthinking adherence to commercial and "middle class values"[27] which is examined in one way or another, in all Wain's fiction.

Wain's moral statements are invariably grounded in the contemporary English scene. All the novels contain sociological descriptions of houses populated by different classes of dingy streets of similar stung-out shops which lead out of industrial cities of one kind of squalor in grimy pottery towns of another kind of squalor in mews flats in Chelsea. A number of the short stories even depend primarily on sociological accounts of contemporary phenomena: the emotions in the kind of love affair on which "the refined moon of Kensington" shines in "Rafferty," the way the young television repairman tries to impress the Swiss fair girl in "Christian at Rillingham." Although references to specific places and to specific attitudes within society are constant throughout Wain's fiction, there is some change in the values assigned. In the first two novels the moral point involves a kind of acceptance of the dominant patterns of contemporary society. Both Charles Lumley and Edgar Banks find a great deal to satirize and castigate and accept, at least on the outside, the kind of class and social role demanded by their time, place and training. Both have learned that genuine value is purely personal; both have acquired sufficient insight to realize that a social position expresses only the outline of a person; but both still accept for its limited worth the expected social position.

In fact, although Wain demonstrates "the value and the importance of the humane,"[28] he also indicates that it is often difficult to understand and explain what human personality is like. Joe Shaw is baffled by what he sees in the people around him. Edgar Banks in *Living in the Present* often cannot understand his own reaction and wonders why irrational fears attack him whenever he tries to carry out his plan. Several of the short stories confront the mystery at the depths of "human personality"[29] even more centrally and directly, using the development of a kind of madness as the representation of all that cannot be understood. The man-boy in "Master Richard" (1960) has to commit suicide at the end of the story because he cannot understand all the intricacies of his strangely displaced personality.

In another story, "Nuncle" (1960), the narrator, a former writer now drinking himself to death, tries to re-establish himself by marrying a placid young girl and moving into her peaceful country cottage. Quite irrationally, he fears his father-in-law who shares the cottage with them. The narrator tries to write again but he cannot write. At the same time, the father-in-law begins to write stories and the two arrange a deal whereby he will write stories under the narrator's well-known name. But the practical arrangement leads to gradual switch in identity; each begins to assume the character of the other and the poor placid girl does not know what kind of allegiance belongs to which man. Finally the narrator must run off to preserve what he can of himself, before identity and personality have been completely swallowed up. "The value of the human,"[30] the limited and the local are not abstractly perfect choices; they are, rather, the only sane possibilities in the midst of psychological complexities that the human being only barely comprehends.

It is true that *The Contenders* has in it only normal situations and normal relationships between people within the framework of normal society. Yet, as Kenneth Allosp opines: "Lamb and Roger are not ordinary—one is supposed to be brilliant artist, the other a brilliant businessman—but at least they are not presented as the psychopaths that their brutal dehumanised conduct would suggest they are." (71)

Yet we cannot shut our eyes to the morality the novel has, particularly the morality that underlines these characteristically happy endings. While analyzing and making a review of *The Contenders,* John Davenport has raised a good point about the way in which critics and reviewers have linked Kingsley Amis and John Wain: "It happened that Wells and Bennett were linked together in the public critical mind, and it has happened to Wain and Amis."[31]

Davenport's statement holds true to a considerable extent as we have already seen in the novel *The Contenders*. With the benefit of hindsight, we can perceive the strain of down-to-earth morality in what Wain was searching for. As William Van O'Connor puts it: "The English school, system, especially from the sixth Form on, demands such an intense competition that the young are marked by it, and some of them spend their lives pursuing goals the inherent value of which they never question."[32]

The moral issue in *The Contenders* is simple and unsophisticated. Wain seems to focus the uselessness of the competitive spirit and the superiority of the value of an older, more local tradition over the dominant patterns of contemporary society.

The concept of humanism of John Wain is his constant commitment to the value of the individual and his constant assertion of the dignity of the human being. Here we discuss the same theme in his two novels—*Hurry on Down* and *Living in the Present.*

II

It was John Wain who set the tone of revolt in his first novel, *Hurry on Down.* The protagonist of this novel is a young man, who "bumps through various sectors of the Post War world,"[33] but he shows no desire to settle down in a "degenerate society"[34] and moves from job to job.

As for the novel *Hurry on Down* and its aspects, let us first take up its plot. The novel opens with a dialogue between Charles Lumley and his landlady. The discourse between the two takes the shape of a verbal quarrel. Lumley wants to abandon the room for good and the lady wants to know the reason for the same. She suspects "he has no prospects"[35] and is therefore worried about his inability to pay his rent. But Lumley must say something to the landlady to make her quiet and stop from any further inquiry. So he tells her that he does the work of a private detective. Still he is not successful in convincing her. The next morning, Charles leaves his room.

Charles has a flashback. He looks back to his university-days. When he was at the university he had shrugged off the question of any of his well wishers by merely saying that he was then busy with his examination and would think of his future with a calm mind. Lumley analyses the reasons of his failure in his life after having the degree. He discovers that he failed because the university had by its three years's random and shapeless cramming crippled his mind for serious thinking. Secondly, circumstances were also responsible for his failure to some extent, and thirdly his problems did not really admit of any solution.

After leaving the house of his landlady, Lumley decides to visit Sheila, his fiancée. When he reaches her house, he finds her away. But Edith Tharkles, her sister, is there along with her "stuffy" (9) husband, Robert. Both are hostile to him. He insults them, and concludes his visit by showering on the greasy water. He, then, goes to a pub and drinks heavily. He is now fully prepared for leading "a completely different way of life."[36] Not surprisingly, Lumley leaves the university and wanders from one place to the other like a rolling stone and never sticks to any particular job. His first job is as a window cleaner. During this period, he lives with Edwin Froulish "a self-advertising pseudo modernist writer."[37] Betty, a "slatternly" prostitute also lives there who supports Froulish. Lumley becomes the partner of Ern Ollershaw, who is quiet about his past. Meanwhile Lumley, per chance, meets Veronica and incidentally falls in love with her, who is living with her Uncle Mr. Roderick at that moment. The words of Veronica are worth quoting here:

> How can you say that? Don't you know that when a woman loves a man she wants everything, everything about him, including what you call burdens—yes, especially those. Can't you see that the only burden to her is to feel that he's keeping something from her?—says Veronica. (133)

A little later, Lumley says to Veronica:

> "Don't you know," he said bitterly, "that when a man loves a woman he wants everything, everything about her and that the only burden to him is to feel that she's keeping." (133)

But in the hospital Lumley has a surprising news that Veronica is Roderick's mistress. He, then, becomes an orderly in the hospital. He meets Rosa, a pleasant but rather simple-minded girl. Their marriage would have materialized, had their interests not fallen apart. Meanwhile he has met Mr. Braceweight, a millionaire. Lumley becomes his chauffeur. The new tutor for Mr. Braceweight's son is George Hutchins, a former classmate of Lumley. Lumley fails to stick to this new job. He just cannot "get on well"[38] with George Hutchins. He then becomes a bouncer in "a combination nightclub and whorehouse."[39] This is followed by a job as a gag writer for a radio show. At this juncture, Veronica appears. Though Lumley loves her even now, he "recognizes that she is the form his new captivity will take his new cage."[40]

Thus, Charles Lumley is seen roaming from one job to another. Throughout, Lumley holds that his goal is "to escape all identification with class."[41] Man may discover himself if the feeling of "class designation"[42] does not come in the way. Lumley feels that it is foolish to consider him as the representative of the working class when he cleans the windows:

> He thought as he leaned on the parapet of the town's bridge and watched the tiny brown river drifting beneath it, of all

> the expensive young men of the thirties who had made or wished to make or talked of making a gesture somewhat similar to his own, turning their backs on the setting that had pampered them; and how they had failed from the start because their rejection was moved by the desire to enter; and be at one with a vaguely conceived people, whose minds and lives they could not even begin to imagine and who would in any case had they ever arrived have made their lives hell . . . and directed all the English working class. (37-38)

On Lumley's reaction to class-stratification, Fredrick Karl remarks: "Reaction to class stratification is clearly key to Lumley, as it is to Amis's Jim. Lumley comes from the bourgeois and he is imprisoned there by virtue of his education and speech, he does not share its aspiration. Sufficiently educated to desert his own class, he nevertheless rejects the tastes of the effeminate highbrows and the factitious sophisticates. He must accordingly make his own world in which class will not be significant. His aim is to be neutral and classless—emotionally, socially and economically." (224-25)

What is notable is the fact that none of his jobs is of high social order. His job at the hospital may be honourable but, then, that was by way of an escape. He does not fit into ordinary life, although he admits that he would like to do so. Lumley in his various anti-social acts is not a simple rebel against the commonplace and bourgeois, as he says that he never even got into it. It appears that once Lumley found a niche in the society, he would "fit in."[43] In other words, he acts for survival. As Fredrick R. Karl goes on to observe: "His acts, consequently, are ones of survival on any terms that life can suggest; he drifts until he finds something acceptable—writing for a popular entertainer—and then wins what he wants, the hitherto unobtainable girl and monetary rewards." (224)

Thus, *Hurry on Down* seems to have in it what Diana Neill calls "the new trend in fiction to blend Rabelaisian humour, working class life and covert criticism of the established order of things."[44] A similar note is struck in the following comment made by Walter Allen: "When *Hurry on Down* appeared it seemed as though John Wain might be satirist of this period of social change."[45] And again: "For Wain in *Hurry on Down,* the picaresque is essentially the satiric; and in this novel Wain, in his grim and gritty and tough-minded way, is very funny indeed, with the true churlish, curmudgeonly denigrating attitude towards men and institutions." (300)

Like Walter Allen, Paul West also finds the novel markedly picaresque: "John Wain's first novel was an exercise in picaresque; his young man bumped through various sectors of the Post War world; the situations were funny, the settings brilliantly vivid, but the characters were little more than faces in a crowd." (131)

Obviously, all these remarks boil down to one common point that *Hurry on Down* is a picaresque novel. Lumley has the look of picaresque figure when we see him by turns as window cleaner, lorry driver, dope peddler, private chauffeur and night-club bouncer. He has his "final metamorphosis as the keyman in a syndicate that provides jokes for comedians."[46]

Incidentally the jobs of Lumley did not have much significance and yet surprisingly he was well paid. The riches he acquired enabled him to get even with the middle class, the established order, which he despised, for its "meanness, pretentiousness and unreality."[47] He made an attempt to be a part and parcel of the working class but all his efforts went in vain. Perhaps Wain must be finding in Lumley his own self when he longed to have the blood of a peasant, the working class which was quite distant from him:

> It is supposed to be rather a trump card to have peasant blood in one's vein, so let me play it, with a flourish. Besides, in England it really is something of reality. English agriculture has not, since the Middle Ages, been in the hands of peasants; the farming has been done by landowners, with a labour force of landless employees.[48]

Lumley's education, upbringing and accent are the hurdles in his becoming a middle class man. Lumley has the aspiration to have both—"to opt out of society and yet to find a niche in it, provided it is one that carries no responsibility of commitment."[49] This may well be seen in the novel towards its end: "Neutrality; he found it at last. The running fight between himself and society had ended in a draw." (488)

Once again it would not be out of place to recall John Wain's words in his autobiography *Sprightly Running: Part of an Autobiography* (1962) when he tells what he wants Oxford to do for him: "Oxford is so deeply in my bones that I am never happy for long away from it. I have no claims; I don't want Oxford to do anything for me to find a niche that fits me to contribute to my support in any way." (96-97)

No doubt *Hurry on Down* has in it some seeds of a picaresque as we find the hero stumbling from "one situation into another."[50] Plot-wise, the novel is done round a central character; incidents get unified solely because they happen to him. This is mark of the characteristically picaresque kind, and *Hurry on Down* is undoubtedly a case in point. To quote James Gindin: "[It] is mock-picaresque. The hero, Charles Lumley, leaves the university and journeys through contemporary Britain, holding successive jobs as window washer, smuggler, hospital orderly, chauffeur and bouncer in a shoddy night club." (128-29)

The plot relates to the theme and is also closely linked with the main characters—chiefly, Lumley, who moves from one job to another to "resist any of the badges of status by which Englishmen recognize one another."[51] But the novel hurls an attack on those who weigh themselves on the balance of class structure or "those who commit themselves to class."[52] That is why Wain makes a vitriolic attack on Lumley through the mouth of Burge, a young doctor, when he surprisingly finds Lumley as a hospital orderly:

> That sort of work ought to be done by the people who are born to it. You had some sort of education, some sort of upbringing, though I must say you don't bloody well behave

> it. You ought to have taken on some decent job, the sort of thing you were brought up and educated to do and leave this bloody slop-emptying to people who were brought up and educated for slop-emptying. . . . If you take a job like that, you've just—'he fumbled among his small stock of metaphors, and brought out the inevitable; letting the side down. And I don't like people who let the side down. (165-66)

Now Wain's "exasperated fury"[53] at the world may remind one of Smollett. Finding Lumley moving from one job to another rather hurriedly, Kenneth Allosp opines: "*Hurry on Down* certainly set a new cycle in recrudescence, of the intellectual rebel without a cause wandering through the deserts and jungles of the Post War World trying to find somewhere to pitch his tent." (76-77)

The rambling of Lumley from one job to another signifies a deep probing into human experience which may eventually lead to a frank and bold exposure of suppressed motives as well as their effects on behaviour. Thus John Wain, like Andre Guy de Maupassant, Emile Zola, Arnold Bennett and John Galsworthy, seeks for the novel a social function what Ibsen and George Bernard Shaw did for the play. If Galsworthy selected the upper class, Wain, like Bennett, opts for the middle-rung class ladder though sometimes like George Robert Gissing's hero, he makes Lumley to be in contact with the working class. Lumley makes an attempt to mix up with the working class when he goes to his old school headmaster for getting a job. The headmaster thinks that Lumley wants a teaching job but he is not interested in a teaching job. Rather, he is interested in a job like window washer. Therefore, the headmaster is surprised. He feels that education has unfitted Lumley for anything worth doing. So he says to Lumley:

> I can only conclude, Lumley, that you felt some kind of grudge against me that impelled you to come back and waste my time with this foolish joke. Window cleaning! I suppose the implication is that your education has unfitted

> you for anything worth doing, and you seek to drive the point home by coming here with this foolish talk about having turned artisan. (30)

It is not the headmaster alone who feels the job is unsuitable for Lumley. Others also ridicule it. "The man with the big face" (109) thinks Lumley is only cracking a joke saying he is a window-cleaner. But when Lumley persists, he shouts: "What's this, a joke about window-cleaner? So that's what you take the little lady [Veronica] away into corner for, is it? You want to tell her stories of that nature. . . . He laughed delightedly." (111)

It is something interesting to find contrary to other's opinion that Lumley by becoming a window-cleaner, thinks he has got a new life. His feelings have been summed up in these words: "He seemed to have been doing it all his life: perhaps in all but a literal sense that was true. His life had only really begun a week ago. Until then, he had merely been an offshoot, an appendage, a post-script, to the lives of several other people. This new life was really his own." (24)

It sounds rather ridiculous when it is known that Lumley is calling at Bunder for a job thereby involving himself into a racket. And the money, which he aspires from the job, is simply for getting Veronica back.

Hurry on Down seems to illustrate the idea that an English "liberal education is a poor preparation for getting on in the world."[54] "The absence of the old style bourgeois,"[55] among whom the hero was supposed to have been brought up, also strikes one when one goes through the novel. Thus, Lumley feels a "sense of isolation,"[56] of the artist-intellectual in the contemporary society. This sense of isolation resembles the kind one encounters in Kafka. In the latter, one finds that nightmare has become a reality and the "individual is trapped in a world, not merely hostile to him personally, but apparently."[57] What is noteworthy is the fact that it is "impervious to human action."[58] Wain at least accepts the decadent aspects of the society where in he finds himself—a gesture which even the giants of the age like Joseph Conrad, D.H. Lawrence and James Joyce rejected. In this connection Arnold Kettle's words are worth quoting: "In even the greatest writers of the age Conrad, Lawrence, Joyce—the battle of the novelist with his raw material tends to be unequal one. None of these writers tamely accepts the decadent aspects of the society in which they all find themselves." (65)

Wain through Lumley is able to achieve a philosophy and hence an artistic vantage point from which he is able quite satisfactorily to cope with and subjugate the world he tackles. So, unlike Conrad, Lawrence and Joyce, he has the confident relaxation of Henry Fielding and Leo Tolstoy. His hero Lumley, like Sartre's heroes, reacts negatively to the easy formulations and obstructions he sees around him and thus seems to be an angry young man. For him, as for Sartre and Albert Camus, freedom is, in a way dreadful and absurd. To quote James Gindin: "The individual has the freedom to act, but he must act in a highly complex and difficult world with little assurance about the value or consequence of his action. That he must act when he knows so little is dreadful." (235)

Hurry on Down, a novel of conduct and class, may be regarded in the English tradition of Richardson and Fielding who dealt extensively with "class distinctions and struggles in eighteenth century society."[59] Samuel Richardson's works are largely the reflection of the man himself. He is a professed teacher and an embodiment of the religious earnestness of the rising Puritan middle class. The virtue he advocates is typically utilitarian rather than fanatical and its reward is material prosperity. Thus the main female character of his first novel *Pamela* or *Virtue Rewarded* (1740) named Pamela marries her wicked master and prospers in the world as a direct reward for her virtue.

In the Victorian age, Dickens, Trollope and Hardy, too, have almost the same theme in which a young man from the lower middle class attempts to enter a more urbane and cosmopolitan society. About the class line, Gindin observes: "Class lines, throughout the eighteenth and nineteenth centuries, were not prescribed with absolute, immutable rigidity, although the problems and the stresses holding back the young man of energy were invariably greater than the opportunities before him." (3)

Hurry on Down, however, depicts a society of somewhat "greater mobility in which the hero is apt to be a good deal less sure of from what or to what he is moving."[60] About the basic problem of the novel of class and conduct (*Hurry on Down* is one such novel) Gindin has to say: "The basic problem of the novel of class and conduct, the issue of how the hero can come or not come to terms with himself and his flexible world, is the same it was during the eighteenth and nineteenth century. But the terms themselves are vastly different and in a society in which change seems to accelerate geometrically, the tone also seems significantly different from that apparent in earlier fiction." (3-4)

Wain in *Hurry on Down* came to the realization "values and alternatives in society were becoming far less fixed and secure."[61] It was probably owing to the fact that the values of conduct and class were rapidly showing signs of a change. The novel, therefore, shows an inclination to centre on personal and metaphysical issues. Wain is very much like Arnold Bennett who was more interested in demonstrating a general theory about time than in dealing with conduct and class. His novel *Old Wives' Tale* (1908) is a detailed social document that is full of human warmth and sympathy. The novelist Arnold Bennett, is interested in giving a realistic account of the lives of ordinary people. He has an eye for detail, an unfailing interest in human life, intuitive understanding of character and a freedom from any ideological aims or bias that place him high as a realist. He has warm sympathy for the poor, but he has strong dislike for the narrowness of English provincial life.

Earlier in the twentieth century when novels did not deal with class, they tended to see class issues from the spectacles of the vanishing intellectual aristocracy, for example E.M. Forster's *Howard's End* (1910) and Virginia Woolf's *To the Lighthouse* (1927). Wain in *Hurry on Down* also seems to attempt to return to a traditional nineteenth century theme: "the theme of how a man works his way through society, with a characteristic twentieth century lack of assurance about what the man or the society is really like."[62]

III

Living in the Present was published two years after the publication of *Hurry on Down* when John Wain was only twenty-nine years old. It would appear that the novel has its genesis in Wain's suppression of his sexual desire in his twenties and also his assuming "a holier than thou attitude."[63] When his father introduced Wain to a man working for one of the big Insurance Companies who had a daughter, Wain had a queer passion. He was expecting a "Big Thing"[64] to come. But as ill luck would have it, it could hardly help being the "Big Thing." The man with his wife and daughter came and all were introduced to Wain. Wain could not pick up intimacy with them and he went straight to his self-constructed cell and slammed the door behind him. Not that Wain did not fulfil the passion. Like a normal man fallen in love, he also had tension. As he writes:

> There is no point in describing the tensions—the day dreams, the sleepless nights, the agonies and exaltations triggered of microscopic incidents, the pleasing declarations, self-abasements and general dog-like devotion . . . it lasted unusually long and unusually virulent.[65]

Wain suffered inwardly. As for the consequences his own confession is noteworthy: "I became hypocritical, a prig, and an emotional liar. Confronted with sexual recklessness, I conveniently forgot about my own unhealthy fantasies and assumed a holier than thou attitude."[66] Perhaps Wain was signally lacking in the right kind of feeling and respect which alone could disinfect one against hypocrisy. Almost all the boys except one or two, he was associated with, were quite innocent so far as sex was concerned. And Wain, on this point, thought himself holier than and superior to those boys though he felt it was an act of hypocrisy as he confesses on making entries into his diary:

> My diary entries are almost incredible even to me. . . . I accepted him as a companion; the minute he translated our talk into action, I raised hands and eyes to heaven. . . . I did not see it with the eye of honesty as a merely undignified affair of pointless nagging and scene making.[67]

So, the result as Wain himself has admitted was "disastrous."[68] Perhaps conventional morality was responsible for it as it would inhibit the "people's happiness." (82) In all probability that is "the price humanity pays for conventional morality. (82)

All the same, Wain feels the necessity of the same for gaining confidence in one's life. He accepts it further:

> But there is equally no doubt that it would have given me a much needed confidence knitted up the two halves of my mind, broken the spell that kept me—wavering on the edge of life instead of plunging in. (82)

John Wain substantiates his argument by narrating an incident in his life:

> I saw this very clearly a little later on, when I went up to Oxford. Most of us were nerve ridden virgins, but there were one or two who had been kicked in at the deep end (one, I remember had been 'seduced' by his Latin mistress at School). You could pick these youths out immediately; these were less worried by life, more pleased with themselves, than the rest of us. (82)

Such was the mental tension John Wain was passing through when he was in his early twenties. He was hypocritical as "he had been at seventeen." (82) Wain could easily see that those boys were far happier than the other boys but "he could not have been brought to admit it." (82-83) All this has a good impact on Wain when he wrote his second novel *Living in the Present* where he gives what he calls "a hostile sketch of a woman corrupts a sixth former." (83) Towards the end of the novel it is found that the woman is persuaded to part with him by "an appeal to her better nature." (83) Finally it is seen that the protagonist is going back to his job as a school teacher and to the "dreariness of his daily living."[69]

The plot of the novel is not a complicated one. Edgar Banks, a schoolteacher finds his life dull and boring. Out of frustration he wishes to commit suicide. Perhaps it is because he finds "no value in his society."[70] Besides, he has the feeling that he belongs to the "second generation of universal agnosticism."[71] But in order to leave the world a little better he chalks out a plan to finish Rollo Philipson-Smith, "a man with a storm trooper mentally."[72] But before doing so, Edgar has some "choices on moral ground."[73] He makes up his mind that before doing so, he will make the world free from "the most loathsome creature he knows"[74] as he thinks: "Who is there among my acquaintance of whom it could truthfully be said that the world would be a cleaner place without him."[75] But Edgar's first attempt to kill Philipson-Smith proves futile. He then follows him and his foolish Scotch follower McWhirter to Switzerland. Banks tries many a time to assassinate him there too, but gets no success. The idea of committing suicide and making the world free from the most loathsome creature continues to be there in his mind as days roll on and he fails many a time in carrying out his mission: "His desire to be rid of the world had not faded, the idea of taking a passenger with him still seemed an excellent one, and Philipson-Smith the best candidate."[76]

All these look what William Van O'Connor feels as "lifted from Sherlock Holmes's stories."[77] Banks's hope of living life is kindled when he meets Mr. and Mrs. Crabshaw and their children, an English family moving to Geneva to improve their standard of living. This is further revived when Banks meets Mirabelle, an American journalist, who goes to bed with him but fails to rid him of his twin obsessions, murder and suicide. This remains for another woman to achieve. The other woman is Catherine who is the fiancée of Tom Straw, the old friend of Banks. Banks falls in love with Catherine but when he is convinced that he cannot have her, he comes back to England. Catherine has also developed a sort of fascination for him and soon she joins him. It develops that Catherine, in fact, is not in love with Tom and is thus free to return Banks's love and that Tom does not love her either. So everybody is relieved. Over and above all this Banks has his "good fortune"[78] that he gets back his school job. "The nihilist," as O'Connor finds, "had begun to live when he had decided to kill himself." (46) He learns how to engage life and finally to affirm it by "sudden inspiration"[79] and thereby make an attempt to enjoy "every hour of life."[80]

But Edgar kills neither himself nor his victim. Something comes in the way at every critical moment in a plot "mocks the serialized cliff hanger and Edgar's automatic response is to preserve life."[81] He is very near killing his victim but his yell for saving a child falling from the tree saves him. He is a failure when he is driving his victim over a hilly road. But it is in all this pursuit that for the first time he seems to be "living in the present open to all emotions and reactions, but uncommitted to any scheme or cause of conduct beyond that of rubbing out his victim and himself. [82] However, to his surprise Edgar Banks meets Tom Straw, his always admired old friend. Catherine, Banks's girl friend, is with Tom Straw. It is here that Edgar Banks feels "that some people with illusion or false good, get beyond the present."[83]

In the process emerges a new personality of Edgar. From some angle he definitely feels "a constant assertion of the dignity of the human being,"[84] though Edgar is seen sometime isolate and depressive. Here he seems very much like Saul Bellow's heroes who are cut off from those who love them. There is, for instance, Joseph in Saul Bellow's *Dangling Man*, who can talk only to himself and that fact accounts for the form of the novel as a journal, the proper form for an isolation. It appears that for this theme of "the dignity of man,"[85] Wain has on him an impact of the theme of Dostoevsky's *Novella*. Like Alexey Velchaninov, Edgar is burdened with guilt. To each comes a "double"—a projection of his guilt nature—whom Edgar and Velchaninov have hurt in the past. Like Velchaninov, Edgar rejects these doubles. The victims—Rollo Philipson-Smith and Trusotsky—prey on the guilt-ridden heroes with a combined hatred and love. Trusotsky tells Velchaninov that he had loved him and looked up to him. Edgar fails to carry out his twin obsession of murdering Rollo Philipson-Smith and committing suicide as "it would mean never seeing Catherine again."[86]

Though there may be a close resemblance between the two novels, yet Wain has written his own novel, not only in the creation of an English urban environment, but especially in its development of the theme of human dignity.

The wisdom of Edgar is that human life has dignity. It has greatness and beauty—the only condition being that it be human life, not subhuman or more than human. It is this dignity of human life that ultimately prevents him from committing suicide. His own statement "death destroys men,"[87] speaks of the dignity of the human life. Wain's sincere realization of this nobility in human life is a positive aspect of the theme, which is at the centre of the novel.

IV

Our discussion on the novels of John Wain in general and *Hurry on Down* and *Living in the Present* in particular leads to the conclusion that he is basically a humanist. Humanism, as Wain advocates, is to know and realize the despair, troubles and sufferings of the people in society, and to attempt to preserve the dignity and value of his fellow beings. A novelist presents the portrait of a (real or fictitious) world of his characters and gives a shape to its theme according to the ideology and mental make-up the author possesses. In whatever situation the protagonist of a novel is placed, he moves only in the direction the author wants to lead him. Viewing the novels of John Wain from this point of view, Charles Lumley and Edgar Banks are true representatives of his ideology and outlook. Though Lumley belongs to the educated commercial middle class he has sympathy for the working class, therefore he takes up manual and menial jobs. In addition to that Wain also wants to uphold the dignity and traditional values which is clear from Lumley's liking for Rosa's father but his disliking for Stan. It reflects Wain's sympathy for the working class and his attachment to the traditional values as well.

Edgar Banks (*Living in the Present*) is placed in a chaotic world lacking value, honesty and integrity. Banks's idea of committing suicide as well as his attempt to kill Philipson-Smith represent the negative approach to tackle human problems. But at the end of the novel, Banks comes to realize the greatness and beauty of human life, he is fully convinced that death is not an escape but destruction of life. Thus John Wain's message to the humanity is that one must preserve one's life as well as the lives of other people.

NOTES

1. James Gindin, *Post-War British Fiction: New Accents and Attitudes,* p. 128.
2. *Loc. cit.*
3. Emile Legouis and Louis Cazamian, *A History of English Literature* (London: J.M. Dent, 1967), p. 1412.
4. *Ibid.,* p. 1430.
5. *Ibid.,* p. 1412.
6. Walter Allen, *Tradition and Dream* (London: Penguin, 1971), p. 300.
7. John Wain, *Hurry on Down*, pp. 37-38.
8. C.B. Cox, *The Free Spirit* (London: O.U.P., 1963), p. 159.
9. James Gindin, *Post-War British Fiction,* p. 138.
10. C.B. Cox, *The Free Spirit*, p. 159.
11. *Loc. cit.*
12. *Loc. cit.*
13. John Wain, *The Contenders* (London: Macmillan, 1958), p. 195.
14. Q.D. Leavis, *Fiction and the Reading Public* (London: Chatto and Windus, 1965), p. 73.
15. John Braine, *Writing a Novel* (London: Eyre Methuen, 1974), p. 47.
16. James Gindin, *Post-War British Fiction,* p. 130.
17. James Gindin, "John Wain," D.L. Kirkpatrick, ed. *Contemporary Novelists* (IV edition, London: St. James Press, 1986), p. 842.
18. Jack Lindsay, *After the Thirties* (London: Lawrence and Wishart, 1950), p. 11.
19. Arnold Kettle, *An Introduction to the English Novel* (London: Hutchinson, 1962), p. 162.

20. Kenneth Allosp, *The Angry Decade: A Survey of the Cultural Revolt of the Fifties* (London: Peter Owen, 1964), p. 15.
21. Fredrick R. Karl, *A Reader's Guide to the Contemporary English Novel* (London: Thames and Hudson, 1972), p. 221.
22. James Gindin, *Post-War British Fiction*, p. 139.
23. John J. Clayton, *Saul Bellow: In Defence of Man*, p. 76.
24. Saul Bellow, *Herzog* (New York: Viking 1964), p. 98.
25. John J. Clayton, p. 76.
26. John Wain, *The Smaller Sky* (London: Macmillan, 1967), p. 86.
27. James Gindin, *Post-War British Fiction,* p. 133.
28. *Ibid.*, p. 139.
29. *Loc. cit.*
30. James Gindin, *Post-War British Fiction*, p. 140.
31. William Van O'Connor, *The University Wits and the End of Modernism* (Southern Illinois University Press, 1963), p. 48.
32. *Loc. cit.*
33. Paul West, *The Modern Novel* (London: Hutchinson, 1967), Vol. I, p. 131.
34. C.B. Cox, *The Free Spirit,* p. 158.
35. O'Connor, p. 44
36. *Ibid.,* p. 45.
37. *Loc. cit.*
38. O'Connor, p. 45.
39. Fredrick R. Karl, p. 225.
40. O'Connor, p. 45
41. James Gindin, *Post-War British Fiction*, p. 129.
42. *Loc. cit.*
43. Wilson Colin, *The Age of Defeat* (London: Victor Gollancz, 1954), p. 83.
44. Diana Neill, *A Short History of the English Novel* (Ludhiana: Kalyani, 1971), pp. 400-1.
45. Walter Allen, *Tradition and Dream,* p. 300.
46. Diana Neill, *A Short History of the English Novel*, p. 401.
47. *Loc. cit.*
48. John Wain, *Sprightly Running: Part of an Autobiography* (London: Macmillan, 1962), pp. 211-12.
49. Gilbert Phelps, *The Novel Today.* (London: Penguin, 1963), p. 488.
50. Rayner Heppenstall, *The Fourfold Tradition* (London: Barrie and Rockliff, 1961), p. 214.
51. James Gindin, *Post-War British Fiction*, p. 129.
52. *Loc. cit.*
53. Walter Allen, *The Novel Today* (London: Longman Green,1960), p. 34.
54. O'Connor, p. 44.
55. *Loc. cit.*
56. Arnold Kettle, p. 64.
57. *Ibid.* p. 65.

58. *Loc. cit.*
59. James Gindin, *Post-War British Fiction,* p. 2.
60. *Ibid.*, p. 3.
61. *Ibid.*, p. 4.
62. *Loc. cit.*
63. John Wain, *Sprightly Running: Part of an Autobiography*, p. 81.
64. *Ibid.*, p. 79.
65. *Loc. cit.*
66. *Ibid.*, p. 81.
67. *Loc. cit.*
68. Edmund Wilson, *The Splendours and Miseries of Evelyn Waugh* (New York: Classics & Commercials, 1950), p. 298.
69. O'Connor, p. 135.
70. James Gindin, *Post-War British Fiction,* pp. 131-32.
71. John Wain, *Living in The Present* (London: Macmillan, 1967), p. 6.
72. O'Connor, p. 46.
73. James Gindin, *Post-War British Fiction,* p. 132.
74. *Loc. cit.*
75. John Wain, *Living in the Present,* p. 8.
76. *Ibid.*, p. 183
77. O'Connor, p. 46.
78. *Loc. cit.*
79. J.W. Cross, *George Eliot's Life* (1885), Vol. II, p. 285.
80. E.M. Forster, *Notes on the English Character, Abinger Harvest* (1936), p. 10.
81. James Gindin, *Post-War British Fiction,* p. 132.
82. *Loc. cit.*
83. *Ibid.*, p. 134.
84. *Ibid.*, p. 139.
85. James Gindin, "John Wain," p. 843.
86. John Wain, *Living in the Present,* p. 208.
87. *Ibid.* p. 154.

Chapter III

Iris Murdoch

This chapter is primarily devoted to an analysis of the theme of humanism in the novels of Iris Murdoch. She is a literary artist who has a purpose which lends significance to her realistic presentation of life. It is in this sense that Iris Murdoch is called a humanist.

Iris Murdoch's training in philosophy plays an important part in her novels, which have a central concern—the "ethical and moral alternatives of the English middle class."[1] A frequent theme is that love is rare and only possible when a person realizes that someone beside himself truly exists. Some critics complain, however, that the philosopher sometimes triumphs over the novelist, reducing her characters to puppets thrown into situations to make a point. But almost all the characters in the novels of Iris Murdoch seek some form of definition, some means of coherently explaining what they are. In her fifth novel *A Severed Head* (1961), the primitive human creature is avoiding the traps and generalizations. The most a human being succumb to, is given a forceful, dramatic bizarre presence in the figure of honour Klein. In the midst of a group of Urban Londoners, characters should drift into and out of numerous love affairs, who constantly define and redefine themselves and their emotions. Honour Klein, an Anthropology don at Cambridge, represents a primitive, permanent human force that all the characters no longer recognize in themselves. He is a representative of primal humane force. In this novel, there are multiple buildings of love affairs, of human relationships detailed extensively to demonstrate human efforts. "Human actions and aspirations"[2] are represented in the houses and the structures human beings build as well as in their attempts to cultivate the land. Imber Court in *The Bell* (1958) represents the clean and pure existence, its inhabitants want to live in order to gain religious meaning and direction.

The response of Murdoch's characters to community is complicated by the paradox of their personalities: although her isolated characters long to be "part of a familial, social or national group."[3] They are at the same time solipsists who rely chiefly on will, ego and power in order to manipulate the behaviour of others according to their own systems and belief. Where there is a power there can be no community. Murdoch's concept of community is realized, therefore, only within "a nexus of morality, imagination, selflessness and love."[4]

Iris Murdoch's repudiation of the retreat from disorder has led to her creation of various images of man-made order as alternatives for isolation and versions of community. Among these, the more important are such social patterns as work, erotic involvements, family entanglements and the restricted inner space of houses within which relationships are explored and confined. In the first instance, work substitutes for community in three ways that serve to illuminate both character and theme. First, the vocation to which an individual is drawn in some cases reflects his psychological inadequacy to give order and meaning to an otherwise vacuous life. Anna's work with the Miming Theatre in *Under the Net* (1954) suggests her need to fit herself into the theoretical world of Hugo Belfounder in order to win his approval and love. Second, work might reflect a character's demonic need to control and exert power over other. Such an elusive and magical character as Mischa Fox, the newspaper magnate in *The Flight from the Enchanter* (1955) is supposed to have at his disposal dozens of enslaved beings of all kinds whom he controlled at his convenience. Third, work can also serve as a means for a protagonist to redeem himself and to work his way towards self-discovery. The change in Rosa's jobs in *The Flight from the Enchanter* from factory worker to journalist and in Jake's jobs in *Under the Net* from hack writer to hospital orderly are creative artist's methods to measure their movement towards selflessness and becoming creative artists in their own right.

Though Iris Murdoch has defined the highest art as that which reveals and honours the minute random detail of the world and reveals it together with a sense of its integrity, its unity and form. The mission of Murdoch is noble and plausible. She believes that literature provides an education to picture and "comprehend the human situation."[5] And yet, in her novels, ideas are far more real than they are in other contemporary novels. The basic idea seems to be "centuries of humanism"[6] that have nourished an unrealistic conception of powers of the will. We have gradually lost the vision of reality separate from ourselves and we have no adequate conception of original sin.

Murdoch believes that the "inner world is parasitic upon the outer world"[7] and that love, far from being redemptive, is in fact the most dangerous of all delusions. It is bound up helplessly with egoism and personal fantasy, the tissue of self-aggrandizing and consoling wishes and dreams which prevent one from seeing what there is outside one.

The human condition is the business of the novelist today and it is Iris Murdoch's too as philosopher and novelist. Of course the Greeks in general always took a fairly grim view of the human situation. She repeatedly cites Plato's feeling that life is not anything much and that human affairs are not serious though they have to be taken seriously. She is not a religious believer, nor a Marxist. She declines as an artist, to serve society in its own interest.

Lionel Trilling writes in *Sincerity and Authenticity* (1970), who would say of himself as Henry James did that he "loved the story as story."[8] Iris Murdoch can say so and her enthusiasm for a story is stronger than even the most recent novels. What Brendan says about taking human affairs seriously is based on Murdoch's reading of Plato and is the best clue to her characteristic adjustments between closeness to life and intellectual detachment. Her role has been to create significance despite the bare humanism of philosophy after Nietzsche. It has not meant trying to write fiction like the Victorians but dealing with what she finds usable in the older novel to create her own imaginative version of our world.

As a philosopher, Iris Murdoch sees the twentieth century individual's dilemma as one in which there is "far too shadowy and flimsy an idea of human personality."[9] In essence, the reason she gives for this circumstance is that modern man has lost moral referents. He has faced and has been overawed by logical positivism, determinism, behaviourism and utilitarianism and has come to believe that reality is merely a quantity of material atoms:

> We no longer use a spread-out substantial picture of the manifold virtues of man and society. We no longer see man against a background of values of realities which transcend him. We picture man as a brave naked will surrounded by an easily comprehended empirical world. For the hard idea of truth we have substituted a facile idea of sincerity . . . we have bought the liberal theory [of personality] as it stands because we wished to encourage people to think of themselves as free at the cost of surrendering the background.[10]

Her handling of personal relationships always distinguished by an acute and often agonizing sensitivity, which is perhaps her outstanding quality, is predominantly romantic in almost all her novels. Though the romanticism is often tempered by an element of the bizarre either in the nature of the relationship or in the circumstances in which it occurs, in her fifth novel *A Severed Head*, it erupts in outright comedy. That the personal problems of her characters and the situations in which they find themselves may be analyzed in terms of internal and external freedom is true enough. But from now on the human experiences are antecedent to the ideas they express. The bizarre and the tragi-comic exist in their own right and fantasy after all is of the stuff of most human beings.

Iris Murdoch attempts to be more precise about the processes by which we, historically and personally, arrive at experiences of freedom, virtue or beauty. She wrote in 1970:

> When I was young I thought, as all young people do, that freedom was the thing. Later on I felt that virtue was the thing. Now I begin to suspect that freedom and virtue are concepts which ought to be pinned into place by some more fundamental thinking about a proper quality of human life, which begins at the food and shelter level.[11]

In her essay "The Sublime and the Good" (1959), she comes to define freedom and virtue as in some ways identical—and they are related to beauty because they are related to the kind of formal truth speaking of the artist. In relating to virtue, she says:

> Virtue is not essentially or immediately concerned with choosing between actions or rules or reasons, nor with stripping the personality for a leap. It is concerned with really apprehending that other people exist. This too is what freedom really is; and it is impossible not to feel the creation of a work of art as a struggle for freedom. Freedom is not choosing; that is merely the move we make when all is already lost. Freedom is knowing and understanding and respecting things quite other than ourselves. Virtue is in this sense to be construed as knowledge and connects us so with reality.[12]

In Iris Murdoch's thought, attention is connected to Kant's concept of attention or respect for the moral law, which is a kind of suffering pride which accompanies, though it does not motivate the recognition of duty. It is an actual experience of freedom. It is such attention which causes Iris Murdoch in "'One God' and 'Good'"[13] to be able to write: Freedom is not strictly the exercise of the will but rather the experience of accurate vision which, when this becomes appropriate, occasions action.

Iris Murdoch's own discussions of the process of attention to moral goodness are conducted with the assumption that such attention will bring with it a sense of where goodness, truth and reality are neither subjective nor arbitrarily open to the election of the will. Her most powerful discussions of the term 'attention' have become part of the technical language of literary criticism; realism, fantasy and naturalism. She says in her book entitled *The Sovereignty of Good:*

> I would suggest that the authority of the Good seems to us something necessary because the realism required for goodness is a kind of intellectual ability to perceive what is true, which is automatically at the same time a suppression of self. The necessity of the good is then an aspect of the kind of necessity involved in any technique for exhibiting fact. (66)

A little earlier in the same book, she has said:

> One might start from the assertion that morality, goodness is a form of realism. The idea of a really good man living in a private dream world seems unacceptable. Of course a good man may be infinitely eccentric but he must know certain things about his surroundings, most obviously the existence of other people and their claims. The chief enemy of excellence in morality is personal fantasy: the tissue of self-aggrandizing and consoling wishes and dreams which prevents one from seeing what is there outside one. . . . One might say here that art is an excellent analogy of morals, or indeed that it is in this respect a case of morals. We cease to be in order to attend to the existence of something else, a natural object, a person in need. We can see in mediocre art, where perhaps it is even more clearly seen than in mediocre conduct, the intrusion of fantasy, the assertion of self, the dimming of any reflection of the real world. (59)

In terms of the relationship between aesthetics and moral Iris Murdoch's descriptions of the objects of fictional attention are instructive. She claims that true goodness is almost impossible to be clear about in life. It can be discerned in art and we can build an aesthetic and moral vision from attempting to understand the precise nature of the excellence of Leo Tolstoy and above all William Shakespeare. To these great writers she ascribes a quality which she initially names 'tolerance' or 'agnosticism.' She later gives the name love to this quality. She writes in her essay "The Sublime and the Good":

> Art and morals are with certain provisions . . . one. Their essence is the same. The essence of both of them is love. Love is the perception of individuals. Love is the extremely difficult realization that something other than oneself is real. Love, and so art and morals, is the discovery of reality. What stuns us into a realization of our supersensible destiny is not as Kant imagined the formlessness of nature but rather its unutterable particularity and most particular and individual of all natural things is the mind of man. (51)

It is true that the theme of humanism and morality is discussed in each of the novels of Iris Murdoch but here we discuss this theme in her two significant novels: *The Bell* and *The Black Prince*.

II

The Bell is probably the best novel of Iris Murdoch. It is a realistic novel full of symbols. The title of the novel itself is a potent symbol. The Bell lies drowned in a lake of a convent, the legend stating that it flew there miraculously. It is the still centre of a complex of human problems, the chief of which is summed up in the character of Michael Meade. He is the founder of a lay religious community and a manor house named 'Imber Court' on the family estate, where the convent is also situated. Meade has suffered a conflict between his homosexual tendencies and his desire to become a priest. The Community, he has founded, is intended to be a way out of the conflict, a compromise and a compensation but he leaves the truth of the maxim to leave the world. But it is not to leave temptations of the world. The novelist says in the novel about Michael Meade: "He has been guilty of that worst of offences, corrupting the young: an offence so grievous that Christ Himself had said that it were better for a man to have a millstone hanged about his neck and be drowned in the depth of the sea."[14]

There are other characters all faced with the need to probe the limits of personal morality to ponder the best means of ordering one's life by abiding essential rules of following *Under the Net* way of existential living so that one is ruled by the situation itself. Dora and Toby are impelled to drag the bell out of the lake and then to ring it; it is the voice of love but also the cast metal of self-realization.

In the novel the inhabitants of the religious Community cultivate a market garden as one of their most important projects. Here the garden is an image for the conscious direction man attempts to give his experience. The garden work for some time thrives and is profitable, but it does not outlive the collapse of the Community that created it. Only the wilderness survives the failure to place the bell on the tower; the wilderness and Dora, the femaleness, flourish. Michael notices: "He watched Dora turning towards life and happiness like a strong plant towards the sun, assimilating all that lay in her way." (335)

The central episodes of the plot in *The Bell* concern the substitution of the medieval bell (legendarily supposed to have flown from the Abbey Belfrey into the lake when a nun had a lover) for the new bell. It is decked to enter the Abbey as a bride and open a new kind of speech between enclosed silent religious order and the outside world. The bell represents art—it is engraved with characters from the life of Christ, who are Iris Murdoch's real other people—squat figures—solid, simple, beautiful, absurd full to the brim with something which was to the artist not an object of speculation or imagination. The words of Nick are worth quoting in this context:

> "Who knows what they expect to achieve?" said Nick, "I'm sure they don't know themselves. Publicity perhaps. I told you this place was appealing for funds. And if you think it sounds mad, it's no more mad than believing that Jesus Christ was God and died to redeem our sins." (266)

Michael Meade, who with his sense of destiny in his call to priesthood or his imaginative vision of moral situations when he falls in love with Nick as a boy and kisses impulsively Tobby, is tempted towards a neurotic vision. Convention is represented by James Tayper Pace who finds it easy to say that some things are simply forbidden and close to moral argument. Michael Meade and Dora in the novel are unpredictable precisely because several outcomes are possible to their dilemmas. In other words, they are free characters.

For Iris Murdoch, there are basically two kinds of people. There are some for whom life is desperate. They are deeply committed to whatever they are engaged in and they can see nothing else. In their steadfastness, they may become grim and morbid. Then there are others for whom life has not settled into any fixed pattern. They are flexible and mobile, desirous of variety and willing to make changes. In the first group, we have Michael Meade, the leader of a lay religious Community located near an Anglican Order of Nuns. In the second group, there is Dora, an easily distracted young wife of Paul Greenfield, a female Jim Dixon, who comes to the Community with her young friend Toby Gashe. But she always does have the feelings of guilt. The novelist expresses the feelings of Dora in the following words: "Dora Greenfield suffered from guilt and with guilt came fear. She decided at last that the persecution of his presence was to be preferred to the persecution of his [Paul Greenfield, her husband's] absence." (7)

The conflict in part of the novel concerns the relations of the spirited, sensual and intellectual Dora with her husband and later with the Community whose spirit is so completely different from her own. In the novel, Iris Murdoch expresses her views of Dora in the following words:

> She was still very young, though she vaguely thought of herself as past her prime. She came of a lower middle-class London family. Her father had died when she was nine years old and her mother with whom she had never got on very well, had married again. When she was eighteen she entered the Slade School of art with a scholarship and had been there two years when she encountered Paul. The role of an art student suited her. It was indeed the only role she had ever been able to play whole-heartedly. She had been an ugly and wretched schoolgirl. As a student she grew plump and peach-like and had a little pocket money of her own, which she spent on big multi-coloured skirts and jazz records and sandals. At that time which although it was only three years ago now seemed unimaginably remote she had been happy. Dora, who had so lately discovered in herself a latent desire for happiness, was the more dismayed to find that she could be neither happy with her husband nor without him. (7)

Dora's attitude represents this world while the Community's are a microcosm of the other. The clash between the two is inevitable and Iris Murdoch chooses to define the conflict in terms of burlesque—a practical joke will demonstrate Dora's need for self-expression at the expense of the Community. The joke centres around a bell, a bell that comes with a legend from the past. In the legend, the bell of the then Benedictine order of Nuns fell into the lake on account of the Bishop's curse. The curse itself derived from the infidelity of a nun and her refusal to confess. When the bell flew into the lake, the guilty nun, overwhelmed by the demonstration of God's power of punishment, flew from the Abbey and drowned herself in the lake.

The present community at Imber Court is planning to install the bell of its own and it occurs to Toby Gashe and Dora that a bell they have located at the bottom of the lake should be substituted for the new one. The one at the bottom they feel, is the bell of the legend.

Running parallel to this course of action in which Dora seeks fun in order to escape from her boorish and possessive husband, is the attempt of Michael Meade to find his own depth without destroying himself. Tempted by young men until he forgets both his principles and his position, Michael is tortured by the knowledge that what he wants, he cannot have. Earlier in his career he had wanted a young boy Nick Fawley and that venture had ended in embarrassment and dismissal; now he sees and wants Toby Gashe and Michael again is unable to resist. There runs through his position in the Community the disparity between his public and private life. He tries to be a good man—he does not have an ideal of behaviour—but his emotions preclude his aspirations.

Michael, the spiritual leader of the Community who takes his turn preaching the weekly sermon, is something of a figure of fun. His passionate twists and turns in which emotions are directed first to God and then to young men parallel those of Dora, who is both attracted and repelled by her husband. Her marriage is just such a combination of duty and discipline, on the one hand, and a need to break out into chaotic excitement on the other. At the time of her marriage, she saw the quality of nobility and integrity in the character of her husband, Paul Greenfield: "She married him for certain integrity and nobility of character which she saw in him." (8)

But her dreams are shattered very soon. She is young and smart and always wants to have the company of her husband. On the other hand, her husband remains busy in his work. Accordingly they hate each other except in bed and their marriage is a compromise that Dora is unwilling to maintain. But outside of her married life, she is a helping lady to her fellow beings. In her train journey, she helps her co-passenger:

> She got up and said to the standing lady, "Do sit down here, please. I'm not going very far and I'd much rather stand anyway."
>
> "How very kind of you!" said the standing lady. "Now I can sit next to my friend. I have a seat of my own further down, you know. Perhaps we can just exchange seats? Do let me help you to move your luggage."
>
> Dora gloomed with delight. What is sweeter than the unhoped reward for the virtuous act? (17)

Michael Meade also confessed and repented over his deeds. The novelist expresses her views of Michael Meade as follows:

> Michael stood for a while looking at Nick's hand. It was a hand that he knew well. He stepped back and sat down on the grass with his back against the warm stone of the wall. He had thought that Nick's revenge could not be more perfect. He had been wrong. It was perfect now. Hot tears began to rise behind his eyes and his mouth opened trembling. (17)

In the novel Murdoch's sense of humanity and literary symbolism are fused in the study of a declining religious Community and the manor house, Imber Court. She conveys the complete reality of all of the main characters's views of the world. Thus she is commended for the "rich humanism"[15] of her concern for the diversity of man's moral views and also for her insight into the diversity of activity into closed forms of work which make our industrial civilization.

III

Iris Murdoch's novel *The Black Prince* presents the story of a middle aged imperfect novelist, Bradley Pearson, who is in love with the young daughter of a second-rate novelist named Arnold Baffin. Bradley stands accused of the murder of Arnold Baffin and dies in prison after recording what seems to be true to him. According to this record, Arnold's murderer is his wife Rachel. Loxias, the Black Prince, gets Bradley's book published. Arnold's daughter Julian becomes a novelist in course of time. Bradley, Arnold and Julian have their views on art and life but Loxias has the final say. In *The Alexandria Quartet* (1956-60), different artists present Durrell's total and complex attitude. Similarly, in *The Black Prince*, there are various artists looking at life and art differently. Thus, they reveal Iris Murdoch's many-sided approach, her ideal being represented by Loxias.

Bradley Pearson wants to write his magnum opus, the story of his love for the daughter of his rival novelist, Arnold Baffin. He despairs frequently in the manner of Bledyard in *The Sand Castle* (1957) about the impossibility of precise description. He says in the novel:

> How can one describe a human being justly? How can one describe oneself? With what an air of false coy humility, with what an assumed confiding simplicity one sets about it! I am a puritan, and so on. Faugh! How can these statements not be false? Even 'I am tall' has a context. How the angels must laugh and sigh. Yet what can one do but try to. lodge one's vision somehow inside this layered stuff of ironic sensibility, which if I were a fictitious character. . . . How prejudiced is this image of Arnold, how superficial this picture of Priscilla! Emotions cloud the view, and so far from isolating the particular draw generality and even theory in their train.[16]

Bradley Pearson lets himself go through a number of experiences trying to keep his life and art at a safe distance. He says: "Life and art must be kept strictly separate if one is aiming at excellence." (212)

He calls his work a love story. He believes that love and art are interdependent, and both bring happiness. He loves Julian, the daughter of his rival novelist Arnold Baffin. Like Vladimir Nabokov's Lolita, Julian feels over-brimmed with real love for this ageing Don Juan. His vision is totally clouded by the emergence of this phantom girl, having no beauty and maturity. He forgets his duty to his ailing sister Priscilla, his promise to Rachel (the mother of Julian) with whom he has slept and failed as a male and above all his sincerity as an artist to write the great book of art. The black eros haunts him day and night. He feels emotionally surcharged and his passion for her wants to break all the frontiers of faith and friendship. He creates situations and pulls the girl into the trap. He elopes with her and intrudes into her innocent virginity. First he fails in performing sexual intercourse. But at last he succeeds violently to his perfect satisfaction on the night he receives the news on phone of the suicide of his own sister. On the same night, Arnold comes and tells his daughter Julian about the death of Bradley's sister and discloses to her that he is actually fifty-eight and not forty-six years old. Julian, who had been bewitched by Bradley previously, is simply bewildered, amazed and shocked. She leaves him and never meets him again. He waits for her to come but she never comes. He murmurs in the last moments of his life in a jail-cell: "Eternally you escape my embrace. Art cannot assimilate you nor thought digest you." (292)

This is his swan song. He leaves his job of Income-tax Inspector to worship the Muses at the shrine of art. He lives waiting for the work of art. Although he, like Jack (*Under the Net*) feels gripped and driven by a sense of destiny. He at last achieves perfection not in life but in death. Death perfects his art.

Bradley Pearson, the novelist-hero of Iris Murdoch, may be compared with Angus Wilson's Bernard Sands (*Hemlock and After* [1952]) who is also a novelist hero. Bernard Sands, like Bradley Pearson, gets the perfection of life in his death. He is a successful writer and self-declared humanist whose message is that one should live according to one's nature. At the climax of the novel, Bernard Sands discovers that his own nature contains elements of sadism which horrify and destroy his beliefs. His wife Ella reminds him of the responsibility for action but Bernard Sands dies having accomplished only a part of what she had argued. The novel ends with Ella's tribute to her husband whom she had only partly known: "My dear," Ella replied, "doing does not last even if one knows what one is doing, which one usually doesn't. But Bernard was something to people . . . lots of people—me for example—and that has its effect in the end, I think."[17]

On the other hand, Arnold Baffin, who is a perfect artist of the second rank, lacks the quality of inquisitiveness. In order to get form in art, he suffers the formlessness in life. Even after his death, his only friend Loxias evaluates him justly:

> But the arts form not a pyramid but a circle. They are the defensive outer barriers of language whose elaboration is a condition of all simpler modes of communication. Without these defenses men sink to beasts. . . . All artists dream of a silence which they must enter as some creatures return to the sea to spawn. The creator of form must suffer formlessness. Even risk dying of it. (414)

Although Iris Murdoch combines the rationalism of Sartre and empiricism of the Britons in her works, yet she preserves her identity as a novelist of distinction. Fredrick R. Karl points out: "What she has presented is a kind of puppet show, created for our amusement rather than for our edification all brightly done, but rather heavily based on existential notions of freedom and necessity and consciousness and unconsciousness." (338)

But it is not a puppet show created for our amusement. Although the impact of existential notions of free will is visible, it is a serious work carefully written on the theme of love. Here Bradley Pearson is under compulsion to write a great work of art. He feels that whatever he is doing is not predestined but it is ordered by a divine power. He writes:

> I felt that every single thing that was happening to me was not just predestined but somehow actively at the moment of its occurrence thought by a divine power which held me in its talons . . . the court room and the judge and the condemnation for life were mere shadows of a much huger and more real drama of which I was the hero and the victim. Human love is the gateway to all knowledge, as Plato un-

> derstood. And through the door that Julian opened my being passed into another world. (389-90)

Again, he says in the postscript of the novel:

> The mechanical aspects of our humanity remain obscure to us until divine power has refined them absolutely and then there is no anxious knower any more and nothing to be known. Every man is tiny and comic to its neighbour. And when he seeks an idea of himself he seeks a false idea. No doubt we need these ideas, we may have to live by them and the last ones that we will abandon are those of dignity, tragedy and redemptive suffering. (389-90)

The outer surface of Bradley's life seems to be disturbed and chaotic, being pulled into various directions. He feels the sense of guilt and expresses his views in the following words:

> How frequent and how bitter is this aspect of human wretchedness. The wicked prosper in front of our eyes and go on and on prospering. What a blessing it must have been once to be able to believe in hell. A great and deep human consolation was lost to us when that ancient and respectable belief faded from our minds. Yet there was more offence even than that something profoundly ugly and repulsive to me: that vision of Roger with his grey hair and his genial pseudo distinguished air of an ageing worldly man holding a girl who could be his daughter, a girl, unused, unmarked and fresh. The particular juxtaposition of youth and age offends, and, I felt offends rightly. (81)

Bradley suffers endlessly. In his childhood, he slept under the counter of his father's shop. His parents died when he was in his twenties. He married and ceased to be married. He had no child. He suffered from intermittent stomach troubles. He left his job of Income tax Inspector. He wanted to save Priscilla, but she committed suicide. He discovered Arnold Baffin and made him a novelist but he hated him. He wanted to sympathize with Rachel when she was hit by her husband but she took a vow to take revenge for seeing her in that state. He loved Julian and she abandoned him. In the last bid, he tried to save Rachel from life-imprisonment by washing and removing the poker with which she had killed her husband and he declares that it is he who has killed Arnold Baffin. He made the death-cell his monastery and Julian his Lovesong. Fredrick R. Karl observes on the ideas of action and love of Iris Murdoch: "She is concerned not so much with self-analysis as with its consequences, specifically with the translation of self-knowledge however imperfect into forms of action really into the act of love. Love is the great mystique, and its forms, she observes with wit and sadness are virtually infinite." (340)

In *The Black Prince*, Murdoch actually translates the self-knowledge of Bradley into forms of action and then into the act of love. Bradley tells Francis about his new transformation into a lover, a worshipper, and feels the hope of reward:

> I've never given myself away before Francis, never gambled myself absolutely. I've been a timid frightened man all my life. Now I know what it's like to be beyond fear. I'm where greatness lives now. I've handed myself over. And it's being under discipline too. I haven't any choice. I love, I worship and I shall be rewarded. (368)

Julian adds in the postscript: "I feel I should in fairness add something else. I think the child I was, loved the man Pearson was. But this was a love which words cannot describe." (411)

Love is the heavenly dew which nourishes the lover in this weary, wild world full of stresses and strains. Love is the bliss in this decaying diseased world. It stirs the artist and awakens him to the light of life. It recreates and makes the lover the creator. It is bliss in curse and a curse in bliss. The only cause of pleasure and pain in this world is a beautiful woman well developed.

Bradley is attracted towards Julian when he sees her bare legs in the shoe-shop. Later on, he develops a craze to see her bare legs. He watches stealthily the under clothes, the breasts and feels enchantingly raptured. Murdoch has mixed the mother-daughter image into one, and the man in Bradley gets fulfilled and destroyed with the bliss and curse of this mother-daughter imagery and out of the debris of Bradley, the man, the artist is born. It is an extraordinary experiment of portraying Bradley as a lover-hater artist, and it is an extraordinary love Bradley confesses of: "After all, I had known this child since her birth. I had seen her in her cradle. I had held her in my arms when she was twenty inches long." (205) And now he holds her in his arms when she is twenty years old, and thinks: "When God said 'Let there be light' this love was made." (206)

Love without sex is like a boat in the stormy sea without a boatman with a strong rudder in his hand. Love and sex have been associated with each other since time immemorial. Love and sex are like the body and soul, like the river and water.

Sex is the creator of the universe. It is not only a biological need, it is the ultimate reality of the creator and the only key to the creation. The world is a manifestation of the play of the sex-energy. Bradley admits frankly in connection with his love for Julian: "Sex is our great connection with the world and at its most felicitous and spiritual it is no servitude since it informs everything and enables us to inhabit and enjoy all that we touch and look upon." (245)

Sex creates new beings, human beings or animals, insects, reptiles, birds and other living objects of the earth. Birth brings death. Living objects grow and die. They have a very short span of life. 'A Lily of a day' may be 'far fairer in May' than the 'Oak tree' of three hundred years or a 'violet by a mossy stone half hidden from the human eye' may attract the attention of a poet like William Wordsworth, but these too have to perish.

These are transient phases of life. Life creates life of a short duration but art immortalizes the moment of beauty in things animate or inanimate, and the artist is greater even than the creator of life. Art has an eternal and universal value. Leonardo-da-Vinci died long ago, but his work of art—'Monalisa'—goes on smiling mysteriously, enchantingly and she will go on smiling in the same manner forever.

Sex, which helps in creating art, is art itself. The beasts also copulate but they breed the beasts of their own species only. Average human beings enjoy sexual intercourse and multiply their species day and night. But artists copulate to create the work of art which has permanent value. In a common man, when emotion is switched on intellect is switched off, as P.B. Shelley observed, but in an artist, it serves, it helps in knowing the Good and the Bad, the Moral and Immoral. T.S. Eliot, writing on Baudelaire, has observed:

> This means, I think that Baudelaire has perceived that what distinguishes the relation of man and woman from the copulation of beasts is the knowledge of Good and Evil (of moral Good and Evil which are not natural Good and Bad or Puritan right and wrong). Having an imperfect, vague romantic conception of Good, he was at least able to understand that the sexual act as evil is more dignified, less boring, than as the natural, 'life-giving,' cheery automatism of the modern world.[18]

Bradley wants to have a vision of selflessness. He wants to keep his aspiration pure. So, unconsciously, he adores the 'lovely boy' figure in Julian. But his trait shows the sign of Latent homosexuality also. Henry P. Laughin defines this trait: "Homo-sexual interest or tendencies which are hidden often from the individual himself. There is no outward expression of them."[19]

After having full sexual satisfaction, he lies in bed in peace. Julian is really surprised at his sudden emergence of the potency. She asks him tenderly and timidly: "What made you like that, Bradley? The Prince of Denmark, I suppose." (329)

Iris Murdoch, one time a Marxist like Doris Lessing and a strong advocate of Sartre, Kierkegaard and other members of the Existentialist Group, seems to be confronted here in this novel with the problem of religion. Bradley Pearson declares in the beginning quite confidently: "Though I am a creative person, I am a puritan rather than an aesthete." (19) But towards the end of his life, he confesses the transformation and change in his vision:

> I felt that every single thing that was happening to me was not just predestined but somehow actively at the moments of its occurrence thought by a divine power which held me in its talons. At times I felt almost as if I were holding my breath in case some tiny movement of my own should therefore with the course of this divine possession. . . . All great truth are mysteries, all morality is ultimate mysticism, all real religions are mystery religions, all great Gods have many names. (390)

Bradley suffers from a perpetual sense of guilt. He seems profoundly repentant on the death of his sister. When his lies are exposed to Julian, he feels repentance for not telling her the truth himself. When he kisses Rachel and finds that he is being watched by Julian, he feels a sense of guilt. In his relation with Julian, a sense of betrayal to his friend Arnold Baffin haunts him. Christian, his ex-wife, also confirms this trait of feeling guilty in him. He is often haunted by a profound sense of guilt. These Christian traits are not absent in him.

IV

In our discussion of the two novels of Iris Murdoch—*The Bell* and *The Black Prince*—humanism is found, as we saw, in various forms, such as the realization of guilt and repentance for the same, helping attitude and sympathy for the fellow beings, her depiction of love as the sublimation of humanity and art as the source of permanent value. All the central characters of *The Bell* and *The Black Prince* have these qualities in them. Dora Greenfield, Michael Meade and Bradley Pearson commit mistakes and suffer for these, and finally realize their guilt. Although Dora does not receive proper attention from her husband, she does not disassociate herself from her husband, thus she suffers a lot. Likewise Michael Meade, who is the founder of a religious Community at Imber Court, suffers from the dilemma: the conflict between his ideas to fulfil his homosexual tendencies and his desire to become a priest. Bradley Pearson suffers because he fails to fulfil any of his desires in life satisfactorily: his marriage was a failure, he could not help his ailing sister, and even Julian leaves him forever.

The central characters of Murdoch's novels have the helping attitude and sympathy for fellow beings. Dora becomes very glad when she helps others, her offering of her seat to a co-passenger is one of such instances. Michael Meade establishes the religious Community at Imber Court and shows his sympathy for other fellow beings. Similarly Bradley Pearson helps Arnold Baffin and other members of the family. He helps his sister Priscilla though he could not save her life.

Love is the nectar of human life, it is a sublime thing. The theme of love has been fully explored and used in the novels of Iris Murdoch. Dora wants to install the bell for the love of her Community members, Michael Meade is very prompt and he never misses his religious sermon out of his love for other people. Bradley Pearson takes love as bliss. He thinks it as the creator of the universe and regards it as the ultimate reality and the only key to creation. Art, Bradley Pearson, thinks is a source of permanent value which immortalizes the artist.

Thus the sense of the realization of guilt and repentance for the same, sympathetic view for others, love for the fellow beings and immortal art may be regarded as the parts which form the humanism of Iris Murdoch.

NOTES

1. Dedria Brytonski, ed., *Contemporary Literary Criticism* (Michigan, 1979), Vol. II, p. 364.
2. James Gindin, *Post-War British Fiction,* p. 185.
3. Dedrie Brytonski, p. 386.
4. *Loc. cit.*
5. Ibid., p. 389.
6. *Loc. cit.*
7. *Loc. cit.*
8. Lionel Trilling, *Sincerity and Authenticity* (London: Rinehart and Winston, 1970), p. 134.
9. Iris Murdoch, "Against Dryness," *Encounter*, XVI, Jan. 1964, p. 16.

10. *Ibid.*, p. 18.
11. Iris Murdoch, "Existentialists and Mystics," W.W. Robson, *Essays and Poems Presented to Lord David Cecil* (London: O.U.P., 1970), p. 179.
12. Iris Murdoch, "The Sublime and the Good," *Chicago Review* XIII, Autumn, 1959, pp. 269-70.
13. Iris Murdoch, *The Sovereignty of Good* (London: Routledge, 1970), p. 67.
14. Iris Murdoch, *The Bell* (London: Chatto and Windus, 1958), p. 108.
15. Alasdair Clayre, "Common Cause: A Garden in the Clearing," *TLS*, August 7, 1959, p. 264.
16. Iris Murdoch, *The Black Prince* (London: Chatto and Windus, 1973), pp. 55-56.
17. Angus Wilson, *Hemlock and After* (London: Secker and Warburg, 1971), p. 246.
18. T.S. Eliot, *Selected Essays* (London; Faber and Faber, 1951), pp. 428-29.
19. *The Neuroses*, p. 990.

Chapter IV

WILLIAM GOLDING

"Nobel laureate William Golding is not only a great writer but also a relentless ideologist. It is widely admitted that Golding is 'difficult' in a variety of ways. His prose is simple. His narrative structures are never obscure or excessively intricate. His characters seem deceptively familiar. And yet, he remains something of an enigma. Critics often add to the difficulties of interpreting a Golding character by evolving their own terminology to cope with it"[1] are the words of Vrinda Nabar expressed before interviewing William Golding during his visit to India in 1987.

Golding as a novelist is greatly concerned with the nature of evil. He considers it in the Orthodox Augustinian way to be built into humanity and redemptible only by those witnesses of grace whom we call saints. On one of his novels *Free Fall* (1959), he takes the theme of conflict between Original Sin and human choice. Sammy Mountjoy, a painter, tells his agonized story from the viewpoint of a man being interrogated by the Nazis. Here choice, free will, good and evil become commodities as actual as "the taste of potatoes,"[2] and Sammy Mountjoy looks back through time at a pattern of evasions, wrong choices and failures to understand. All day long action is weighed in the balance and is found neither opportune nor fortune but good or evil. The narrator is muddled as real human being.

Not only is William Golding concerned with the nature of evil, he is also preoccupied by the evil in man's soul. It is there in the depth of the soul. In his first novel, *Lord of the Flies* (1954), the young and innocent schoolboys chant: "Kill the beast! Cut his throat! Spill his blood!" That demand seems to symbolize the unredeemable impulse in history.

William Golding shares with most of the modern novelists an anxiety about modern civilization. It is their constant endeavour to help man by lifting his heart and making him aware of hope, honour and pride which is the glory of a human being. In their novels, they are at their best where they wish that men in some degree suffer and conquer where they admit to be being humanistic. The novel, nowadays, stands around a humanistic concept of the world. Graham Greene, Evelyn Waugh and William Golding are the major recent Christian novelists while Angus Wilson and William Cooper are the agnostic humanists. All these Christian novelists believe in a source of value beyond this world and can hope for grace in the struggles of life.

William Golding, like other Christian novelists, represents the modern world largely in negative ways. He is generally obscured with plight of fallen man with the spirit in man's mind, the insidious attraction of evil and the insidious attraction of good. The sinfulness of man is his essential emphasis and he tries to work out salvation for his characters through his religious commitment.

Though William Golding, unlike Graham Greene and Evelyn Waugh, is not a Roman Catholic, he is regarded as a religious writer. In this context, Peter Green's words are worth quoting: "Golding is primarily a religious novelist; his central theme is not the relationship of man to man but the relationship of the man individual to universe; and through the universe to God. . . . He represents himself theologically as what used to be loosely termed as Deist."[3]

The whole moral framework of Golding's novels is concerned in terms of traditional Christian symbolism. His essential emphasis is on the sinfulness of man. His first novel *Lord of the Flies* shows painful authority and the destructive potentiality of human beings. He tells the story of a group of English boys who survive a plane crash on a tropical island. The boys were apparently evacuated during a destructive atomic war and are left with no other control anywhere about to build their own society on the island. They chance to create a new paradise is clear enough, but Golding quickly indicates that the boys are the products and intrinsic parts of current human society.

Golding's second novel *The Inheritors* depicts the story of the last family of man's ancestors conquered and supplanted by man. The family migrates to its spring home and slowly realizes that things have changed, and discovers the encroachments of a tribe of others. The "people"[4] are not capable of thinking of abstractions. They simply act by instinct and 'have pictures' many of which they do not understand. Yet for all their perpetual and intellectual limitations 'the People' have a code of ethics, a deep and humble sense of their own limitations and a faith in the divine power and goodness of the earth which undoubtedly makes the theme of the novel humane. Golding's different metaphors employed in his novels can be read as orthodox and traditional Christian statements about the nature of man. Each metaphor underlines man's depravity, pride and the futility of his reason. The novels are permeated with the sense of man's sin and guilt and the images depict these qualities in conventional Christian terms.

His next novel *Pincher Martin* (1956) is a tremendous study of a torpedoed sailor's lonely struggle for survival on a rock in the mid-Atlantic. It is a religious novel. Pincher's friend Nathaniel is a mystic who talks: "of the technique of dying into heaven. Take us as we are now and heaven would be sheer negation. Without form and void. You see? A sort of black lightning destroying everything that we call life."[5]

But Christopher Martin Pincher in the naval slang which conveys his moral character is not really interested in heaven. He is to find himself later recalling this conversation, exposed on the rock, declaring ironically: "'I am damned if I'll die!' At the very last Martin is searching for a kind of peace and feels the black lightning playing over his crab-like self with a compassion that was timeless and without mercy."[6]

The novel has thus entered an imaginative realm far away from our normal experience. But the process by which Christopher Martin becomes Pincher the crab is seen in the terms of a humanistic morality. It is not his rejection of God but his selfishness towards men has been emphasized. Flashbacks reveal Christopher's life in the theatre as an actor using people to further his career.

On the rock, Martin realises what he has done to himself: "Because of what I did I am an outsider and alone." Nathaniel is the person he loves disinterestedly but wrecked by jealousy, he decides to murder Nathaniel: "Good bye Nat, I loved you and it is not in my nature to love much. But what can the last maggot but one do? Lose his identity?" Thus at the end Martin recognizes a sound as "the grating and thump of a spade against an enormous tin box that had been buried." (129) The eater is about to be eaten. The novel is full of morals, and humanists will find no difficulty in accepting it.

The Pyramid (1967) consists of three stories told in the first person about life in a small provincial town, beginning between the wars. We are given three pieces of Oliver's life and the title implies that they may be seen in a meaningful relationship. The first concerns the adolescent Oliver's romantic love for the inaccessible Imogen and his first sexual experience with the local "easy girl, Evie Babbacombe."[7] It culminates several years later when Oliver is an Oxford undergraduate and Evie reproaches him with his selfish exploitation of her young body. He seems to have made a profoundly humanistic discovery about the relationships through Evie and perhaps to be in a position to develop now beyond the selfishness of adolescence towards a more mature attitude. Oliver takes part in the performance and is befriended by the professional producer, Evelyn de Tracy, a man of sensitivity and intelligence who is well aware of the phoney social role he plays. Oliver is warned in a pub by his friend not to speak openly of his ambition. He wants to know the truth of things but is unable to find it. When in reply Evelyn shows him his photographs as a young man in a ballet skirt, Oliver roars with laughter, totally unaware of Evelyn's distress. Returning to the theatre for the last act, Oliver listens the song of Imogen.

The final section takes place after war when Oliver, now married and with two children, returns to Stilbourne in a new car. He gets petrol from the garage belonging to Henry Williams. In retrospect Henry's achievement of success is shown to have been built on the exploitation of the spinster music teacher Miss Dawlish, who had loved Henry and helped him generously. Henry had used her to develop his career and commemorated her when she died with an impressive grave with the inscription "Heaven is music." (174)

Throughout the book, music suggests values higher than materialism. For a while, Oliver had worked seriously with Miss Dawlish, "a time for me of peace and delight in which the sky over Stilbourne lifted to an infinite distance." (196) But poor schoolwork in science caused his parents concern and he agreed to concentrate on getting to Oxford. He achieved this successfully at the expense of an important part of himself. If the figure on which the novel is based, is a pyramid, it is one in which success for one person is built on the exploitation of others.

The social observation is accurate but we find a fatalistic view of human personality lying beneath it. The epitaph 'Heaven is music' has proved a lie, for music could not help Bounce when human beings failed her, but it does represent a value in the novel which the characters deny at their peril. Oliver's choice of success through science rather than taking the risk of becoming a musician has involved the sacrifice of a part of his nature. Golding's world is a grim one and there is no hint in *The Pyramid* of a God other than Henry's 'god without mercy.'

The unusual settings of several of his novels, the Pacific island of the school boys in *Lord of the Flies*, the Neanderthal world in *The Inheritors*, the Atlantic rock in *Pincher Martin* and the medieval world of *The Spire*, show how far Golding is from offering the kind of realistic observation of normal society which is the central tradition of the novel. Mark Kinkead-Weekes and Ian Gregor in their *William* Golding: *A Critical Study* (1967) used the term 'history' for this aspect of his novels. They argued that Golding's development could be seen as a movement between two other aspects namely from the clear formulations of the 'fable' to the profounder implications of 'myth'. Humanistic writers have been mainly concerned with 'history.' Golding's consistent claim is that he wishes to go deeper. He says: "If he has a serious, an Aeschylean, preoccupation with the human tragedy, that is only to say that he is committed to looking for the root of the disease instead of describing the symptoms. I can't help thinking that critics of the Aeschylean outlook are those who think they have an easy answer to all problems simply because they have never looked further than the rash appearing on the skin."[7] The question which this claim prompts is whether Golding's novels follow through the investigation of the 'disease' in a spirit of humane concern.

Lord of the Flies shows with painful authority the destructive potentiality of human beings. The experience of the boys in the island is certainly a paradigm of human situation, and it ends with the decent boys being hunted to death by the aggressive hunters. The last minute rescue of Ralph by a British naval officer turns into an irony as the officer's eyes dwell on the 'trim cruiser in the distance,' a weapon of war more efficient than any Jack has been able to contrive. At this point we have invoked the idea of Original Sin and thought that the sinfulness of man is Golding's essential emphasis. What Ralph weeps for at the end is "the end of innocence, the darkness of man's heart and the fall through air of the true, wise friend called Piggy."[8] This is an exclusively religious awareness which leaves humanists with a facile optimism that would deserve no one's respect. Modern humanism must have something to say in the world of Auschwitz and Hiroshima; it may not talk of sin, but it must admit the destructiveness of which man is tragically capable.

What would distinguish a Christian from a humanist view of these matters would not be the diagnosis but the suggested treatment. The Christian believes in a source of values beyond this world and can hope for grace to help in the struggles of life. The humanist can have no such hope. Here we find a direct conflict with Angus Wilson vis-a-vis Christian humanist with agnostic humanist. In fact, Angus Wilson is an agnostic humanist and has no faith in any source of values beyond this world. A striking scene in the novel occurs when Simon confronts the pig's head which the hunters have placed on a stick in the hope of propitiating the Beast to whom they attribute their misfortunes. The head, known as the Lord of the Flies, appears to Simon as an enemy and speaks to him with the voice of a bullying teacher:

> "What are you doing out here all alone? Aren't you afraid of me?"
>
> Simon shook.
>
> "There isn't anyone to help you. Only me. And I'm the Beast."
>
> Simon's mouth laboured brought forth audible words. "Pig's head on a stick."
>
> "Fancy thinking the Beast was something you could hunt and kill!" said the head . . . "you knew, didn't you? I'm part of you? Close, close, close! I'm the reason why it's no go? Why things are what they are!"
>
> The laughter shivered again. (158)

Simon is regarded as a saint in the novel. It is he who is killed when he brings the other boys the good news that what they had taken to be the Beast was merely the body of a dead airman caught in the branches by the lines of his parachute. But in fact Simon's good news is highly rational. His assertion—'Pig's head on a stick'—is a courageous denial of the head's view of itself: 'I'm the Beast'. What the head goes on to assert is only realized by Simon. He realizes that the evil, which is destroying the once happy community, comes from within humanity itself. But it is too late, Jack and the hunters have already chosen the life of killing and guilt, projecting their own impulses on to an external being, whom they now seek to propitiate. There could be no more rationalistic account of the origins of religion. The world of *Lord of the Flies* suggests the existence of no power beyond humanity likely to help in solving the problems of human society and relates these problems directly to the rejection of reason. In a recent monograph on Golding, Paul Elmen criticizes the inadequacy of Golding's view of evil: "He does not sufficiently realize that the evil is outside man as well, so that man not only projects evil, but is also sometimes seized by it, as the Nazis undoubtedly were seized by demonic powers."[9]

William Golding's belief that "man produces evil as a bee produces honey"[10] is at the centre of almost all of his novels. His extraordinary and irrational view is that evil sometimes seizes men who are helpless before it, and can be defeated only by supernatural aid. It throws into sharp relief the rationality of Golding's account of how men may be led by pride, guilt and fear into murder, sadism and disaster. Therefore, he calls them terrible disease of human beings and they aim to make face the sad fact of his own cruelty and lust. Behind their wide diversity of tone and setting lies the fixed conviction that man is a fallen being. He is gripped by Original Sin. His nature is sinful and his state perilous. As Golding has recognized, this is an insight that lacks novelty being obvious and familiar in theological terms. But he contends: "what is there is true and a truism can become more than a truism when it is a belief passionately held."[11] His novels can be seen as an attempt to justify this. However, what he calls his savage grasp on "life appears to be no more than a heavy handed clutching at standard religious props."[12]

Although the theme of humanism is found in almost all the novels of William Golding but the focus of the present study is centred on his two novels—*Lord of the Files* and *The Inheritors.*

II

Lord of the Flies is a religious novel embodying a conception of human depravity which is not limited to the Christian doctrine of Original Sin. The novel is religious because it suggests that its values are more developed and more affirmative than in fact they are. Golding makes no reference to Grace or to Divinity, but only to the darkness of men's hearts and to the God of Dung and Filth. Simon is a saint. The quality of sainthood is a valuable human condition.

The novel also offers a paradigm of the adult world. William Golding thinks that the adult world is a hedge against what children experience in themselves. A Christian morality hangs heavy on the novel from the 'choir boys' doffing of their robes to Jack's tears of repentance and the gaining of self-knowledge. Golding wants to show that evil lurks beneath smooth surfaces, ready to come out, not to make social or political point about children and from them about the adult world.

The metaphor of the society which the boys construct is not left to do its work alone. Just when the savage forces led by Jack are tracking down Ralph and burn the whole island to find him, a British naval officer arrives to rescue the boys. Throughout the novel, frequent references to possible rescue and to the sanity of the adult world seemed the delusions of the rational innocent. Ralph and Piggy often appealed to adult sanity in their futile attempt to control their world. At the end of the novel we find that adult sanity really existed. The horror of the boy's experience on the island was after all a childish game only. The British officer turns into a public school master and says: "I should have thought that a pack of British boys—you're all British, aren't you? —would have been able to put up a better show than that." (248)

The officer's density is apparent but the range of the whole metaphor has been severely limited. Certainly the whole issue, the whole statement about man, is not contradicted as Golding directly points out, Ralph has learnt from the experience: "And in the middle of them, with filthy body, matted hair, and unwiped nose, Ralph wept for the end of innocence, the darkness of man's heart, and the fall through the air of the true, wise friend called Piggy." (248)

But the rescue is ultimately a trick, a means of cutting down or softening the implication built up within the structure of the boys's society on the island. The young heroes of *Lord of the Files* climb away from the dark, scrambling up the pink cliff or wild stuff of their island. The island is their refuge, the only hard and secure place in the midst of the vast stretches of water around them. The novelist expresses it in the following way:

> Wave after wave, Ralph followed the rise and fall until something of the remoteness of the sea numbed his brain. Then gradually the almost infinite size of this water forced itself on his attention. This was the divider, the barrier. On the other side of the island, swathed at midday with mirage, defended by the shield of the quiet lagoon, one might dream of rescue; but here faced by the brute obtuseness of the ocean, the miles of division, one clamped down, one was helpless, one was condemned, one was . . .
>
> Simon was speaking almost in his ear. Ralph found that he had rock painfully gripped in both hands, found his body arched, the muscles of his neck stiff, his mouth strained open.
>
> "You'll get back to where you came from." (122)

Ralph is vaguely aware that Simon's words extend beyond their literal meaning, and he searches his friend's face for a clue. Indeed, the words express Simon's deeper insight into man's condition and echo those of the priest in *Ash Wednesday* (1930). The place, which the little prophet alludes to, is the darkness from which man comes and to which he must inevitably return however strong his grip around the rock.

Just as the island protects the boys from the darkness outside, the conch is their little illusory talisman against the darkness in themselves. After the beautiful and complex object and reverie has emerged from the informal wetness of water and weeds, they hold it firmly in their hands and turn it into a symbol of order and reason. Significantly, the irrational forces that finally prevail make it explode into a thousand white fragments together with rational Piggy's skull. This clearly anticipates the invented rock of Pincher Martin disintegrating under the white lightning. Like Ralph, the drawing officer will grip rock with both hands, but the literal rock to which the child clung in an instinctive gesture to protect himself has become the desperate invention of a man aware of the nothingness awaiting him. The boys's fear is much vague: it comes with darkness and assumes the shape of a mysterious 'Beast' that rises up from the sea, from the bottom of their unconscious, as dim racial memory to which they can give no name.

From the first meeting of Ralph and Jack in *Lord of the Files*, we are made aware of a close relationship between these two twelve years olds: Ralph who had brought the scattered groups together by blowing the conch shell and Jack, the leader of the choristers, appears out of the heat despite Jack's confident claim: "I ought to be chief because I am chapter chorister and head boy. I can sing C sharp," (23) Ralph is chosen leader by the vote of the majority of the castaways. He is everything a leader should be, handsome with fair hair, good build and a natural ability to command. He also holds the conch which becomes the symbol of order, of fair speech and the rule of reason.

Golding implies a close relationship between the two in the last chapter as Ralph lies hidden from the boy hunters who are pursuing him to death. He thinks himself: "Then there was the indefinable connection between himself and Jack; who therefore would never let him alone, never." (203)

Ralph and Jack are complementary to each other, one standing for all that is reasonable, the other the man of action who prefers the killing of pigs to talk. At first, they work together sharing the delight of exploring the island: "Eyes shining, mouths open, triumphant, they savoured the right of domination. They were lifted up: were friends." (32) But soon there are quarrels over the building of shelters and keeping alight the signal fire on the mountaintop. The older boys preferring the immediate excitement of hunting wild pig to the humdrum activities which Ralph and his closest follower Piggy organize: "There was the brilliant world of hunting tactics, fierce exhilaration, skill; and there was the world of longing and baffled common sense." (77)

Golding makes us aware throughout the novel of the erosion of Ralph's authority and its passing to Jack. Jack and his hunters provide meat and involve others in the mimetic ritual of killing the pig with its circular dance, its chants, painted faces and symbolic victim. Eventually, Jack gathers to himself all the boys on the island, except Piggy and Ralph and sits in state on a great log: "painted and garlanded . . . like an idol. There were piles of meat on green leaves near him and fruit and coconut shells full of drink." (164)

He has become almost a god-king, to be worshipped and offered gifts and who in turn holds the power of life and death. A further stage in his coming into his full inheritance occurs after the raid when Piggy's glasses, the source of fire, are stolen.

The conch, a symbol of order, is ignored by the raiders as it depends for its effectiveness entirely on the recognition of its symbolic function. Yet it is only with its destruction and the fall through the air of the true, wise friend called Piggy that all inhabitants are lost by Jack and his followers.

Suddenly Jack bounded out from the tribe and began screaming wildly:

> "See? See? That's what you'll get. I mean that! There isn't a tribe for you anymore! The conch is gone. . . ." He ran forward stooping. "I'm chief!" Viciously with full intention, he hurled his spear at Ralph. (200)

Ralph must die in order that the succession is finally secured, so Jack and his henchman Roger organize the tribe—for we have ceased to regard them as children—to track and kill their former leader. It is only the fortunate arrival of a naval officer and his men attracted by the smoke of a bush fire which saves Ralph from the fate of the pigs. Their heads have already been offered to placate the Beast, the power of evil which the boys feel, is on the island.

If Ralph and Jack display the forces of attraction and repulsion common to opposite poles, then Piggy comes to represent the voice of reason which articulates all that Ralph feels but cannot express himself. Piggy is undoubtedly cleverer than Ralph but he has none of Ralph's assurance nor does he share his popularity. As Peter Green points out: "Piggy is more than a fat, asthmatic, coddled, myopic stubbornly sensible Cockney: he is the voice of sanity personified, a Promethean symbol. It is his thick-lensed spectacles which are used to light the vital signal fire, and are later stolen by the hunters. He will have no truck with group consciousness, but remains embarrassingly individual; and because of that he is killed."[13]

It is Piggy who suggests that Ralph uses the sound of the conch to summon the survivors, who organizes the collection of their names and who appeals for order: "How can you expect to be rescued if you don't put first things first and act proper." (50) He refuses to accept the likelihood of there being a Beast on the island:

> "I don't agree about this here fear. Of course there is nothing to be afraid of in the forest. Why—I've been there myself! You'll be talking about ghosts and such things next. We know what goes on and if there's something wrong, there's someone to put it right."
>
> "You don't really mean that we've got to be frightened all the time of nothing? Life," said Piggy expansively, "is scientific, that's what it is." (91-92)

He states further: "He has a firm and unshakable conviction in adult omnipotence. 'Grown-ups know things. They aren't afraid of the dark. They would meet and have tea and discuss then things'll be all right.'" (103)

Piggy is an outsider throughout the novel and only understood by Ralph but rejected by others in his appeal to man's rationality. In his acceptance of science as providing an ultimate answer, he is very much the exemplar of the attitude that everything is susceptible to reason that was popular in the late nineteenth and early twentieth centuries before it was shattered by two world wars. It is the voice also of Sir James Frazer who in the last chapter of *The Golden Bough* describes the way in which "every great advance of knowledge has extended the sphere of order and correspondingly restricted the sphere of apparent disorder in the world, till now we are ready to anticipate that even in regions where chance and confusion appear still to reign a fuller knowledge would everywhere reduce the seeming chaos to cosmos."[14]

But William Golding cannot share Frazer's optimistic view of the nature of science. He thinks that science is controlled by a corrupt mankind. Thus it is the result of an atomic war from which the boys find themselves stranded on the island. They have the sign of the adult world which is sought by Piggy and Ralph. It descends on the island in the form of a dead airman who brings terror in their nights. Their threefold appeal to reason does not prevent Piggy and the conch is destroyed by the huge rock which Roger levers down upon them:

> "I got this to say. You're acting like a crowd of kids." The blooming rose died again as Piggy lifted the white magic shell. "Which is better—to be a pack of painted niggers like you are, or to be sensible like Ralph is?" A great clamour rose among the savages. Piggy shouted again. "Which is better—to have rules and agree, or to hunt and kill?" Again the clamour and again—"Zup!" Ralph shouted against the noise. "Which is better, law and rescue, or hunting and. breaking things up." (33)

It is Simon who accompanies Ralph and Jack on their first joyous exploration of the island. He also realizes the truth about the Beast, the pig's head spiked on a stick and left as an offering and who in his compassion cuts the corpse of the airman free "from the rocks, and the figure from the wind's indignity." (162) He, alone among the boys, feels the real nature of evil on the island that is not external but part of their selves. As the head says in Simon's delirium: "Fancy thinking the Beast was something you could hurt and kill . . . you know, didn't you . . . what they are." (158) And when in darkness Simon comes down from the mountain—as Christ after the transfiguration—he is set upon in the frenzy of the boys's ritual dance:

> The sticks fell and the mouth of the new circle crunched and screamed. The beast was on its knees in the centre, its arms folded over its face. It was crying out against the abominable noise something about a body on a hill. The beast struggled forward, broke the ring and fell over the

> steep edge of the rock to the sand by the water. At once the crowd surged after it, poured down the rock, leapt on the beast, screamed, struck, bit, tore. There were no words and no movement but the tearing of teeth and claws. (168)

Simon has died in his effort to bring the good news and his flesh is sacrificially eaten after the ritual enactment of the slaying of the Beast. He has become the human substitute.

It is, therefore, fitting that the body of Simon—Golding's Christ figure in the classic mould of the dying god—is claimed by the sea after his death. We are made aware of the affinity between Simon and the natural forces, which move to take him to his rest. The water is dressing his hair. It is silvering his cheek and turning his skin to marble. The phosphorescent creatures are attending his head. His broken body is being lifted with infinite care and gentleness:

> Along the shoreward edge of the shallows the advancing clearness was full of strange, moon-beam bodied creatures with fiery eyes. . . . The water rose further and dressed Simon's coarse hair with brightness. The line of his cheek silvered and turn of his shoulder became sculptured marble. . . . Softly, surrounded by a fringe of inquisitive bright creatures, itself a silver shape beneath the steadfast constellations, Simon's dead body moved out towards the open sea. (169-70)

Another aspect of the dying god which has already been mentioned is the association in death with pigs and bears—quite appropriately for a vegetation deity as pigs are notorious for the damage they can do to any growing crops.

Lord of the Flies deals with Original Sin and a state of alienation from good by which mankind is equally gripped from birth. There would be no propriety in the boys' apparent innocence at the beginning, in the evident continual innocence of Simon and the commonsensical Piggy, nor in the resistance to evil put up by Ralph. These things may be factually compatible with believing that the three also alienated at heart. Again, original sin might lead one to expect some dealing with the mysterious ways out from it which are offered under names like grace and redemption. In *Lord of the Files*, the sense of struggle with something itself whole-heartedly corrupt suggests something different. What speaks through the pig's head sounds analogous to that, namely a power not ourselves, but in ourselves, making for corruption. As the title suggests, the book is about the experience behind the Biblical name for God's adversary, Beelzebub which does indeed mean Lord of the Flies. It is proper enough that the boys who are killed in sacrifice to him should be the innocents.

In the new world of *Lord of the Flies*, Simon is no longer only a helpful boy who liked praying in the forest where Jack finds only terror. Simon called Ballantyne's hero, Peter, 'the Rock' a Christ figure because he has Christ's reward. He goes down from the mountaintop to tell his friends that the thing on it is the fallen corpse of an airman. But he is killed by them because they think he is the Beast. In the world in which they are, humanity confronted by evil, the boys behave with as much fitness as they do if they are considered only as silly little boys.

A naval officer looks down and sees them. In one way, this is a rescue which is properly and ironically accounted for. The boys had tried earlier unsuccessfully to attract ships with the smoke of a bonfire, and now by setting to fire the whole island in an attempt to smoke out Ralph, they succeed. But in another way, the naval officer and his cruiser remind us at the end of the book, like the crash landing of the boys at the beginning and the fall of the airman in the middle that the boys are themselves escaping from a world war. The shift of viewpoint from child to man drives home what we learnt among the children, "Ralph weeps for the end of innocence and the darkness of man's heart." (248)

III

Golding once called himself "a propagandist for Neanderthal man."[15] In his second novel, *The Inheritors*, Neanderthal man is superseded by homo sapiens who have better brains and weapons. But it is the innocence of the doomed predecessor that we see enacted and see the activities of the new man. He is intelligent and capable of evil through the bewildered eyes of the old. And Golding admits that we belong with the new man and supposes that we could not recapture the quality of innocence and natural awe for Oa, the mother goddess.

The feat of recording observations of the activities of homo sapiens made with the sensory equipment of Lok is the astonishing virtuosity. We are always reminded of the involuntary powers that sustain him. His ears speak to him even if he will not listen. The small areas of skin react with the useful knowledge, the nose marvellously distinguishes and identifies. We can always see that the extinction of this animal is necessary where he observes a new man aiming at him with a bow and can no more conceive of what the man is doing than he can impute enmity. It is so similar to a being or explain his tall face—his senses simply report a series of inexplicable events. Lok and the female Fa observe the communal activities of the new people from a vantage point in a tree. This is carried out with a fierce imaginative power that is not in the least inconsistent with a very minute attention to the complicated effect to be communicated. What is shown is that although we are experiencing these events innocently, by way of the passive vegetarian, inhuman senses of Lok. And at the end we abruptly leave Lok, with a loss of sympathy, observe him with our normal sight, joining the new men. With these anxious and responsible technicians we sail away with only a last glimpse of superseded innocence stumbling about on the shore of the dead world.

The Inheritors is a process of man conquering the 'people' and capturing or killing them one by one. The last of the 'people' is able to watch man, to understand dimly man's power and victory. But this last survivor of the people is also able to sense in what ways man is a creature different from the 'people'. He watches man brawl and fight, steal other men's mates, suffer guilt and anxiety, and tear himself apart between his real ability and his failure to exceed his limitations. The novel carries the implication that man's unique power to reason and think carries with it his propensity toward pride, sin and guilt, qualities that cause him pain and misery.

Most of the novel is told from the point of view of the last of the 'people', a humble creature who depicts the issues without fully understanding them. However, the last chapter provides a switch in the point of view, for it is seen through the eyes of one of the men after the 'people', the "devils"[16] in human terminology, have been wiped out. The theme does not change; man sees himself as a being tortured by pride and guilt. He has faith in his power but continually runs into conflict with other men and with his own limitations.

The Inheritors is a remarkable imaginative feat. The task William Golding has set himself is the all but impossible one of showing us Neanderthal Man in his own terms. He succeeds well enough at least to give us a notion of Neanderthal Man that is at once plausible and moving. And through his innocent anthropoids, he shows us man as cruel, evil, and inventive. Evil is equated with knowledge, indeed with being human.

At the beginning there was Oa, the source of all life whom the people revere. The old woman is her living representative, the one who lights the fire, buries the dead and makes the simple ritual gestures of an embryonic religion. Little Oa, a root figuring of a woman's body, is the People's talisman, and their sanctuary is a cavern which has the shape of a womb and is situated at the end of a narrow gully figuring the birth canal. Once Lok creeps with Fa through the gully, but when he sees the blue shadows inside he agrees with his mate that there is "too much Oa for a man" (85) and he experiences a rudimentary religious feeling. Even the people's "pictures" (79) of shells as they climb away from the sea suggest the cave-matrix which is the beginning and end of all things and of which the sanctuary with the glittering ice-women on its walls is the perfect crystallization:

> The caverns where the ivy branches led were their loins. Their thighs and bellies rose out of the cliff above. They

> impended so that the sky was smaller than the floor of the sanctuary. Body linked with body they leaned out, arching over and their pointed heads flashed in the light of the moon. He saw that their loins were like caverns blue and terrible. They were detached from the rock and the ice. The pool of sound had risen to their knees. (84)

In this sacred place the ivy branches, the seeping water, and the women's loins, all bring the source of life itself. The close union of the linked bodies also symbolizes the People's "Oa-ness" (195) with each other and with nature. Their lives follow the natural rhythm of the seasons and the simple cycle of water. As spring advances into summer, they leave the cave by the sea and climb up rocky slopes to their platform near the waterfall. And at the end of their lives's journey, either they resume the fatal position in Oa's belly like Old Mal and Lok or they are dragged back to the sea along the waterfall like the Old Woman and Fa. Death is accepted simply, without fear, as a natural process common to all living things and creatures.

By taking away the log on which the people used to pass on their way upwards, the New Men have cut the umbilical cord that linked them to Oa. They have isolated themselves on an island, and their dugouts have carried them over to a new stage in the evolution of their species. But their emancipation from Nature also engenders insecurity and fear. They sail away from the beasts in the forests, and the vast stretch of water around their island-boat fills them with vague terror as it did the boys on their boat-shaped island in *Lord of the Flies*. Even when the light comes back with the dawn, they remain full of confusion, "haunted, bedevilled, full of strange irrational grief." (224-25) Homo sapiens have tasted the bitter fruit of knowledge and must now pay for it. The immensity of all that remains to be mastered renders Tuami's achievement ironically meagre. He wonders, giving up working at the blade of his ivory-point: "who would sharpen a point against the darkness of the world?" (231) Yet he holds it in both hands, as a weapon against darkness:

> Holding the ivory firmly in his hands, feeling the onset of sleep, Tuami looked at the line of darkness. It was far away and there was plenty of water in between. He peered forward past the sail to see what lay at the other end of the lake, but it was so long, and there was such a flashing from the water that he could not see if the line of darkness had an ending. (233)

The measureless unknown ahead and the irrational fear behind do not have an ending. Tuami and his tribe pass on their craving for knowledge and their fear of the dark to their children and the inheritors of the earth. They climb further and further away from the "cave by the fire," (179) filling the empty gap with whatever torment and terror there is in themselves.

The people do not know anything of art. Their religion is devoid of ritual, though they pray and make offering before Oa, who brought forth the earth from her belly and is present where Awe is. Art and ritual are like conceptualization, a kind of shaping of experience and a projection and division of the self. It is understandable that they should go together But the people have other qualities which seem obscurely connected with these first three. They are like the boys at the beginning of *Lord of the Files*, innocent usually mutually affectionate, excited by their world. They are at home in their forest; and though they are omnivorous, will not eat meat unless something else has killed it and sucked the blood. Even then they feel guilty about it.

Our early ancestors are believers in survival of the fittest and continuous competitive use of weapons. The epigraph from the most brilliant of monuments to the belief in progress, H.G. Wells's *The Outline of History* (1919-20) warns us that the subject of the book is the encounter between homo sapiens and Neanderthal Man. Nevertheless, it is a long time before one is finally convinced that the people through whom we see are Neanderthal Man, and the 'other' people by whom they are at first attracted and eventually destroyed, our own forerunners. Neanderthal Man has something in common with our unfallen ancestors mythically imagined in a reaction against Wells and rationalism similarly to Golding's by C.S. Lewis in *The Problem of Pain:* "All that experience and practice can teach he had still to learn: if he chipped flints, he doubtless chipped them chemsily enough. He may have been utterly incapable of expressing in conceptual form his Paradisal experience . . . if the Paradisal man could now appear among us, we should regard him as an utter savage creature to be exploited or at best patronized. Only one or two and those the holiest among us would glance a second time at the naked, shaggy-bearded slow-spoken creature; but they after a few minutes would fall at his feet."[17]

The unity of some of the qualities of a fable with the method of inner exploration is the special quality of a Golding novel. In *The Inheritors*, as in *Lord of the Flies*, part of the way it is achieved, is the shift at the end. The naval officer's grown-up views in one, and in the other the viewpoint of the Inheritors, Homo Sapiens, our own ancestors. And they, we realize, are unquestionably fallen. Like the boys at the end of *Lord of the Flies*, they kill freely, have hunting rituals and project their own evil on to the forest. They are frightened of the air where there is nothing, says the Neanderthal Woman Fa.

Above all they project their own evil on to the Neanderthalers. When Tuami, the artist among the new men, draws pictures of the first man at the bidding of the witch doctor Marlan, it is Marlan at his most evil they resemble. The hair stood out round the head as though the figure were in the act of some frantic cruelty. The hair of the old man had stood out when he was enraged or frightened. Indeed, Marlan becomes more like his own projected evil side; when we see him through Tuami's eyes. He has acquired the Neanderthaler's red hair and the tense posture and blind eyes of the pictures. The sun was blazing on the red soil and Marlan was red. His arms and legs were contracted. His hair stood out and his beard, his teeth were wolf's teeth and eyes like blind stones and later, in a moment of terror, his eyes were glaring like stones.

H.G. Wells's view of the Neanderthalers is that of the new men: the vision of our own projected evil selves. So far as that view contains facts, it is true even to the cannibalism. The Neanderthalers's old leader Mal asks as he dies: "Do not open my head and my bones. You would only taste weakness." (87) It is evidently nothing sinister, but a posthumous act of love. But the new men eat a Neanderthal girl, Liku, because they are hungry and do not care to eat the fungi and other things the Neanderthalers eat. Golding makes use of a further detail which Wells mentions and which points the other way from the contrast of ogre-like Neanderthalers and amiable Homo Sapiens. The Neanderthaler's teeth were less marked, less like dog-teeth, than ours is the view of Wells. Our teeth that remembered Wolf as Golding's Neanderthalers see them and Marlan's wolf's teeth are seen by Tuami.

But to Wells and to the new men, the Neanderthalers are devils who live in the darkness under the trees. We know the "red creature" (216) is Lok, and see his discovery of the death of Liku. His tears and presently his death, and the projection of evil on to Lok are more pathetic and appealing.

We learn the projection to the mind of Tuami, the artist, and find it bound up with the capacity of the new men to conceptualize and to perform and develop magic rituals that centre round art. The new men can distance themselves; therefore they live in self-deception. Their power of conceptualization is, in short, bound up with their fallenness. In this, Golding is closer than C.S. Lewis to the Biblical myth. For Lewis the Fall can only have been man's wish to exist independently of God "to be on their own, to take care for their own future, to plan for pleasure and for security to have a mews . . . which was theirs not his."[18] Golding pushes fallenness back to the division in the self, the awareness of oneself over against everything else which is the precondition of Lewis's fallen wishes. Fa has dim pictures—that shoots might grow nearer the shelter and water be carried in shells—that approach Lewis's notion. But, she does not have enough detachment from her pictures to see how to do it; and the Old Woman of her people warns her off even from these as if from poison. Golding's Neanderthalers are not divided even from one another. One of the deep silence fell on them that seemed so much more natural than speech. It was a timeless silence in which there were at first many minds in the overhang; and then perhaps no mind at all. The new men only get drunk together, and make savage love. They have done what the "Bible perhaps expresses in the eating of the fruit of the tree of knowledge of good and evil and Adam and Eve first knew that they were naked."[19]

IV

William Golding emphasizes that man is basically sinful because he inherits the Original Sin. Though he has both evil and good forces within him, the former always dominate. However, there are some rare persons with pious souls who work and sacrifice themselves for the salvation of mankind. Therefore almost all the central characters representing human beings do have these traits, that is, they have evil tendencies and are selfish by nature, and want to destroy the happy human community. Every boy, except Simon in *Lord of the Files*, indulges in evil deeds and wants to prove his superiority over others. Similarly, the Homo Sapiens in *The Inheritors* do all sorts of evil deeds and want to prove that they are better than the Neanderthalers in all respects. Thus they represent the evil forces. On the other hand, Simon, the 'Christ figure' (*Lord of the Flies*) and the Neanderthal Man (*The Inheritors*) represent good and innocent forces. The novels of Golding show that a struggle for supremacy is always going on between the good and evil forces within the society (and also within man himself). The death of Simon (representing good and innocent forces) clearly illustrates that it is the evil which ultimately wins the battle.

Apparently it seems that Golding advocates the evil but he does not do it in real terms. In fact, he presents the modern world in negative ways, that is, he shows us what the modern world should not be. Though the symbols and images of Golding are mostly from the world of Christianity, they have their roots in humanity, perhaps the real universal religion. The struggle between good and evil is universal and Golding's treatment of this theme in his novels clearly shows that he is a humanist.

NOTES

1. Vrinda Nabar, "An Interview with William Golding," *The Times of India*, March 15, 1987, p. 6.
2. *Ibid.*
3. Peter Green, "The World of William Golding," *A Review of English Literature,* April 1960.
4. William Golding, *The Pyramid* (London: Faber and Faber 1967), p. 12.
5. Mark Kinkeed-Weekes and Ian Gregor, ed., *William Golding: A Critical Study* (London: Faber and Faber, 1967), p. 129.
6. *Loc. cit.*
7. William Golding, "The Writer in his Age," *London Magazine*, 8 May 1957; qtd. Peter Faulkner, *Humanism in the English Novel*, p. 170.
8. William Golding, *Lord of the Flies* (London: Faber and Faber, 1954), p. 248.
9. Paul Elmen, "Contemporary Writers in Christian Perspective," A monograph on Golding, 1967, qtd. Peter Faulkner, p. 172.
10. Peter Kemp, "William Golding," *Contemporary Novelists,* ed. D.L. Kirkpatrick, IV edition, p. 352.
11. *Loc. cit.*
12. *Loc. cit.*
13. Peter Green, "The World of William Golding," *Transaction and Proceedings of the Royal Society of Literature,* Vol. 32, 1963, p. 43.
14. James Frazer, *The Golden Bough* (Abridged ed., London: Macmillan, 1957), p. 931.
15. Stephen Hazell, ed., *The English Novel* (London: The Macmillan Press, 1978), p. 153.
16. William Golding, *The Inheritors* (London: Faber and Faber, 1955), p. 231.
17. Qtd. Stephen Medcalf, *Writers and Their Works: William Golding* (London: Longman, 1975), p. 75
18. *Ibid.,* p. 17.
19. *Ibid.,* p. 19.

Chapter V

KINGSLEY AMIS

Kingsley Amis is a humanist who treats various human themes on several intellectual and social levels. He expresses passions, pleasures, difficulties and strains of social conditions in his novels. He is also concerned with the problems of individual human beings.

Amis's concept of humanism is essentially connected with the theme of "social adjustment."[1] In his contemporary fictional world morality is simply material and conversational, but it never becomes the issue along which the novel is directed. The theme of the novels is ultimately "adjustment, adjustment of the individual and his aims to the wider society in which he lives."[2] If man faces a world where experience is constantly fragmented and incongruous where no single line of conduct is invulnerable from the ridicule of another point of view, his only possibility is to concentrate on his individual desires and make his way through the world as best he can. In The novels of Kingsley Amis the concept of humanism also centres around his moral preoccupations. His heroes support the Labour Party and are advocates of the Welfare State. Social and moral references abound because man deals with social and moral facts continuously.

The novels of Kingsley Amis emphasize the necessity of good works and show the ways to lead a moral life in the natural world. Although this moral seriousness is only hinted at in *Lucky Jim* (I954), it becomes increasingly evident in *Take a Girl Like You* (1960). Whereas in *Lucky Jim* the values are hidden beneath a comic narrative, the comedy is submerged beneath a more serious treatment in *Take a Girl Like You.* Thus the latter is a turning point for him in a number of ways. Here the characterization is more complex, the moral problems are more intense, and the point of view is not limited to only one central character.

Although Kingsley Amis generally shapes his novels to endorse the value of adjustment, he altered the attitude towards adjustment in the course of his fictional career. Initially in *Lucky Jim* and *That Uncertain Feeling* (1955) the value of adjustment was debatable, although the process is inevitable for a talented young man. In *That Uncertain Feeling*, Amis develops sympathy for the man who is unable to adjust and must retreat to the provincial society he came from. Later in *I Like It Here* (1958) and *Take a Girl Like You*, questions about the value of adjustment become more the matter for superficial comedy and the worth of adjustment. It is just like that of learning to order a meal, drive a car, or lose virginity, is taken for granted. In *I Want It Now* (1968), adjustment becomes a positive virtue, contrasted to the selfish deviations of eccentrics who are eventually exposed. Yet the rightness of the resolution is always casually stated negatively. At the end of *Lucky Jim*, Jim Dixon, less arid and phoney as a teacher than are the other academics, is rewarded because "it's not that you've got the qualifications . . . you haven't got the disqualifications, though, and that's much rarer."[3] Similarly at the end of *I Want It Now*, the hero and the heroine come together acknowledging that they are not quite as bad as others. They can help each other not to be as bad as we would be on our own.

Morality in *Take a Girl Like You* is the subject of incessant debate but does not effect the outcome of the story and yet all Amis's heroes talk a great deal about honesty and integrity. In the novel Patrick exuberantly plays the role of an export-import man in order to impress his expensive woman in London:

> "No," he said, preparing to enjoy himself. "I'm to do export and import. Chemical fertilizers. Disinfectants. Pest sprays. Sheep dip. Cattle dip. Horse dip. Pig dip. Donkey dip. Mule dip. Camel dip. Elephant dip. Llama dip. Buffalo dip."[4]

But the roles are more than material for parody. They illustrate the perspective, the view of man's position in the world that runs through all Amis's novels.

Kingsley Amis is a serious novelist of wide appeal. He is a creative artist whose concern for human values in modern society is inseparable from his interest in the art of the novel. His very first novel earned him the label "an angry young man"[5] which he has not been able to shake off. It also proved him to be the master of comic art. The characterization of Amis as 'an angry young man' is appropriate, but is not quite the whole truth. Indeed, taken by itself, it might detract from a proper appreciation of Amis's creative achievement in the art of the novel. A proper perspective on him should be based on the three coordinates: his social concerns, comic vision and an awareness of traditional moral values.

The comedy of Amis's novels is generally satirical in intention but is enlivened with exuberant laughter. Laughter is used as a main rhetorical device. The targets of the aggressive laughter are usually those social institutions which promote such morals and manners as are prejudicial to the growth of the community of men and women. These institutions are rooted in the stratifications of the contemporary English society in economic classes of the rich and the non-rich. In particular Amis's "comic"[6] intentions seek their fulfilment in exposing the ridiculous aping of the rich by the middle class. The social climbers come from the middle class and their single most significant ambition of life is to be accepted by the self-contained rich. The process of climbing the social ladder involves them into petty dishonesties which are consequent upon their imitation of the moral and manners of the filthy rich. Amis distinguishes between the true aristocrats born to manners and those who are not born to manners but possess wealth acquired through shady means. The full force of his jeering laughter is directed against the nouveaux riches no less than against the social climbers from the middle class. However, while taking due note of the comic speech mannerisms and other idiosyncratic behaviour of the true aristocrat, Amis generally spares them the snarl of the bite of his sarcasm. In other words, his comedy is not the comedy of manners limited to the superficial aberrations of individuals in society, which are treated with facetiousness and light-hearted witticism. His comedy, therefore, is deeply social in inspiration. It is comparable in certain respects to the satirical comedies of G.B. Shaw on the themes of social significance. This is not to say that Amis's comic vision is starkly moral in its main thrust, i.e. it does not seek to educate us in matters of morality, either religious or secular. There is a good deal of moral implicit in his novels but it is the morality of the social tradition based on common sense observation and experiences of the ages. Amis's moral standards grow from his sense of human decency, his generous impulses, liberal sympathies and accommodating spirit. In our opinion it is this set of values that enables Amis to strike a balance between the satirical intentions and exuberant comic spirit. Amis himself underplays the social element in his comedies. He writes:

> I find that sometime the American reviewers found the things I have intended more than the English reviewers. I think the social element in what I write has been largely invented by reviewers here. The Americans do not see it because they don't really know much about post-war England. I'm saying something about modern society, yes, but only in the details. What I'm really interested in is human nature as it's always been, and this is what the Americans understand. But I do feel that there is going to be any background at all you must get it reasonably right, if you set a novel about jealousy in fifteenth century Antarctica it won't mean as much if you set in twentieth century South London.[7]

Amis claims to be a writer of funny books, but on reading his novels one is persuaded to believe that he is a serious writer preoccupied with significant and vital aspects of social life. Kenneth Hamilton has observed rightly when he says: "Amis detests solemnity and protests that his purpose is to write funny books. It is difficult to analyze a good humorist's work without appearing to be intolerably heavy handed. Nevertheless, every writer must be judged by what he produces and not by what he says about his productions; and Amis plainly gives us novels worth close attention. He is a serious writer. His range of interest covers a wide area including politics, contemporary morals and manners, and the abiding relevance of the seven deadly sins. We can hope that he will continue to entertain us. Yet we would be less than grateful and more than obtuse did we not also expect him to keep on being the kind of comic novelist he has proved to be a moralist."[8]

One of the most significant concerns of Amis is rooted in the traditional respect for human decency. There is nothing profoundly metaphysical or religious about the value of decency and fair play in human life. But it is certainly a prime human value which is rightly emphasized by Amis. It is not limited to a given society or a given culture, it is common to all societies and cultures. The moral taboos and prohibitions may vary from society to society, the number of commandments may change from time to time, but the values of sincerity and integrity may safely be considered to be eternal and universal.

In his endeavours to communicate his rational traditionalism Amis is supported by the tradition of the novel to which he claims to belong. To a question as to with which writer he felt the closest affinity, Amis replied: "With Henry Fielding, though it seems a gross impertinence; Anthony Powell, though that might again be considered so; Iris Murdoch. That doesn't mean to say that I want to write like them."[9]

We readily accept the truth of Amis's observation on his affinity with Fielding and Powell. Amis's view of life and reality is as liberal and flexible as is Fielding's. Concern for sane and decent relationship is what they have in common; broad-minded geniality and tolerant good humour characterize them both. Even the affinities of Amis with Anthony Powell are many and quite pronounced, but what is intriguing is his assertion that he has affinity with Iris Murdoch too. Iris Murdoch is a metaphysician of love; she is a neo-Platonist concerned with 'the sovereignty of good.' She is an enlightened Anglo-Irish Protestant deeply concerned with sin and redemption. Amis's affinities with her are so mysteriously deep-rooted as not to be perceptible to us. In our opinion Amis belongs to the tradition of comic fiction inaugurated by Fielding, developed by Dickens, and revived by Evelyn Waugh and Anthony Powell.

Amis, in the modern period, like H.G. Wells earlier, attempts to restore "social"[10] reality to its rightful place in the novel and, therefore, he may be considered to be a 'traditionalist."[11] His conservatism in respect of the form of the novel is continuous with his rational traditionalism in respect of human values that he explores and evaluates in his novels. Thus Amis's formal as well as thematic concerns and his attitude to the relationship between society and individual, distinguish him as a 'Classicist' than a 'Romantic.'

As a true classicist, Amis has full faith in the enduring stability of his society, his sharp criticism of the social institutions notwithstanding. He is well known as a ribald blasphemer, but only he who believes can blaspheme effectively. Amis's attitude to sex and women is rooted in his respect for women. In *Take a Girl Like You* morality, specifically sexual, is the subject of incessant debate. Jenny Bunn is determined to keep her virginity; Patrick is just as determined to take it from her. The argument is often handled in comic terms. Jenny loses her virginity but not as a result of moral or immoral suasion; Patrick tricks her into capitulation while she is drunk. Although moral issues make Jenny periodically resolve not to see Patrick again, and at the end she is able to say, 'Well, those old Bible-class ideas have certainly taken a knocking, haven't they?' Jenny has learned that in order to keep Patrick and to operate successfully in the more sophisticated town, she has moved and abandoned the moral principles she grew up with. Self-interest demands the abrogation of principle and Jenny living in a world different from her parents is no fool. Again the relevance of morality is pushed back into another age for as Patrick explains during one of his earlier arguments with Jenny:

> There used to be a third sort, admitted. The sort that could but didn't—not with the girl he was going to marry, anyway. You'd liked him all right, though and would not have given you any trouble trying to get you into bed before the day. The snag about him is he's dead. He died in 1914 or thereabout. He isn't ever going to turn up, Jenny that bloke with the manners and the respect and the honour and the bunches of flowers and the attraction. Or if he does he's going to turn out to have a wife in Birmingham or a boy friend in Chelsea or a psychiatrist in . . . wherever psychiatrists live.[12]

The so-called irreverence and irresponsibility of Amis towards women and sex are really nothing else than his sense of freedom from the inhibition of social taboos, which must be violated for emotional release. Thus, his art is healthy and promotes sanity of outlook towards morals and manners in society. "'society"[13] is the central concern in Amis's novels.

Indeed, Amis's fundamental concern with the man in society has been made the basis of grouping him with the contemporary rather than with the modern novelist. According to Stephen Spender, the contemporaries are those who are engaged in the exploration of the social and political circumstances of their age. The exploration is accompanied by protest against these circumstances and the attitude expressed is one of optimism in the possibility of improvement for the better. G.B. Shaw, H.G. Wells, Arnold Bennett, John Galsworthy may be included among the contemporaries. On the other hand James Joyce, Virginia Woolf and D.H. Lawrence are among the 'Moderns.' The distinguishing features of the 'Modern' novelists are their acute awareness of an inner crisis of sensibility, a conviction that the nature of this crisis cannot be rendered through the conventional forms of communication and therefore ceaseless experiment with the form of the novel must be carried on in order to express the complexity and the mysterious quality of human situations. The moderns are little concerned with the social and political circumstances of the world they write about. This distinction between the contemporaries and the moderns seems to place greater value on the moderns. They are shown to be the explorers of the complex, depths of human psyche whereas the contemporaries appear to the surface of life.

The novels of Amis are rooted in the "social situations"[14] which are the characteristics of Modern English society. The end of the Second World War marked the emergence of the Welfare Society. The door of higher education was opened to the youths of lower middle class through various scholarships. The young men and women from this class could now enter the institutions of higher learning and prove that they were capable of greater academic achievements than the sons and daughters of the upper class. But the class-ridden British society produced only frustration, disillusionment and consequently anger among this new class of men. They felt helpless against the prevailing social economic inequality and they raised their angry voice against the undervaluation of human intelligence and personal merit. Amis, too, raised his angry voice but he is shown to be different from other 'angry' contemporaries in that his anger is mixed with good-humoured satire.

All the heroes of Kingsley Amis, for example, support the Labour Party and the Welfare State. Yet this support is less a consistent political or social allegiance than the instrument used to puncture the pretence and gentility of others or to conceal the hero's own social embarrassment. Jim Dixon, John Lewis and Garnet Bowen equate their support of the Labour Party with behaving badly, shocking others, and making nuisances of themselves at cocktail parties. John Lewis, surveying the room at a Party, wonders:

> Should I break in a renewed effort to be marked down as 'impossible,' hawl a defense of the Welfare State, start undressing myself or the dentist's mistress, give the dentist a lovely piggy back round the room. Call for a toast to the North Korean Foreign Minister or Comrade Malenkov.[15]

The theme of class relation in English society figures prominently in the novels of Kingsley Amis. We find his treatment of this theme in each of his social novels. What needs to be stressed is that his attitude to it is not of a Marxist revolutionary, demanding complete revolution in the social system nor of an apologist of the system. It is, of course, critical, and the criticism is rooted in Amis's understanding of human moral values. To the extent the class structure is hostile to the normal growth and demands its suppression. It is a common knowledge that economic disparity is productive of unfair evaluation of human intelligence. Persons endowed with greater intelligence and moral perception but suffering from economic privations are unfairly rated as inferior human beings, while those who are poor in intelligence but rich in material possession acquire high social respectability and are treated as superior human beings. In almost all the novels of Amis, to a greater or lesser degree this situation is critically evaluated and the rich are shown in their true colours and the poor are placed in the proper perspective. However, Amis is not angry with all the rich, because they constitute one monolithic class; he has a graded scale of moral discrimination on which he places the rich according to their intelligence, generosity concern for their fellow "human"[16] beings and courtesy to those who do not belong to their economic bracket. His basic intention seems to protect and promote basic moral virtues in human beings regardless of their economic status in the society. He does not spare the representatives of the middle class either from his criticism, i.e. they are also critically evaluated, for the lure of wealth involves them into many subterfuges and compromises which are inimical to their moral being.

Amis seems to take a partisan view of human beings; for him the rich are usually bad and morally ugly, the poor are usually good but subject to harassment by the filthy rich. If even a character who is rich and also good appears in his novels, his existence is very tenuous and his physical presence in the novel rather insignificant. Gore Urquhart and Julius Ormerod are a case in point. It then appears that Amis's attitude to life and human beings is primarily conditioned by the role of economic factors in society. By the same token it may be safely concluded that his interests and preoccupations and his view of human beings are product of his real experience of concrete social reality. His society is primarily secular and its basic concerns are primarily economic. It is a society in which riches are greater good than moral values. Amis is the spokesman of traditional amorality, who satirizes and exposes the amorality of material possession. This is his strength within the narrow range of interest that he explores in his novels. The seriousness of his moral concern is usually lost sight of in the gaiety of his comic spirit that pervades his novels. The tense balance between comic drama and moral concern is the most prominent feature of his creative imagination. His anger is essentially moral, the mode of its expression is logically comic.

Thus it can be seen that the theme of humanism which is connected with the theme of social adjustment centred round the moral preoccupation is found in all novels of Kingsley Amis, but the present study focuses mainly on his two novels—*Lucky Jim* and *That Uncertain Feeling.*

II

The Encyclopaedia Britannica describes ethics as "the systematic study of the nature of value concepts, 'good', 'bad', 'ought', 'right', 'wrong', etc . . . and of the general principles which justify us in applying them to anything also called 'moral philosophy'."[17]

Lucky Jim is a systematic study of 'good' and 'bad'; 'right' and 'wrong' and this view is reiterated by Amis himself. He says that when he wrote *Lucky Jim,* he had something serious to say. Hence behind the comic facade lurks an orthodox believer in the sadness of traditional morality. The protagonist of *Lucky Jim* has a strong sense of pity and responsibility. His mind and feelings are so dominated by the images of those virtues that he finds Margaret Peel attractive than Christine Callaghan:

> Dixon moved closer and saw her hair had been recently washed; it lay in dry lustreless wisps on the back of her neck. In that condition it struck him as quintessentially feminine much more feminine than the Callaghan girl's shining fair crop. For old Margaret, he thought and rested his hand in a gesture he hoped was solicitous on her nearer shoulder. (76)

It is incidentally no accident that pity and responsibility are so much the characteristic virtues of the heroes of *The Heart of the Matter* (1948) of Graham Greene. Pity and responsibility are for Amis white sepulchres, seeming virtues which cover masochism. When Jim thinks that he is doomed to lose Christine and end up with Margaret, in some sense by his own choice: "He remembered a character in a modern novel Beesley had lent him who was always feeling pity moving in him like a sickness, or some such jargon. The parallel was apt, he felt very ill." (185)

It is also typical that the problem is treated pedagogically and that Jim's preceptor is a woman. When he dismisses as adolescent the insistence on sexual desire as a criterion in choosing a marriage partner, Carol Goldsmith disagrees, and tells him:

> after the maturity of my twenties was over, I began going back to that way of explaining things with a good deal of relief. And justification, I'd like to think, too, I'm rather keen on that formula these days, as a matter of fact . . . you'll find that marriage is a good short cut to the truth. No, not quite that. A way of doubling back to the truth. (124-25)

Jim is much impressed: "These things helped to give her presence or solidity and emphasis that impressed him; he felt not so much of her sexual attraction as the power of her femaleness." (123) Amis is claiming here some alliance with that nineteenth century liberal tradition in the novel. And it is notable how often his heroes are instructed and put down at the hands of a woman.

Having learned this lesson Jim applies it to his own attraction to failure. He must find within himself the courage of his own desires. He persuades Christine for a taxi-ride with him, he resolutely stifles his self-punishing impulse to feel that she ought to disapprove the trick by which he procured the taxi for them: "This ride, unlike most of things that happened to him, was something he'd rather have than not have. . . . It was one more argument to support his theory that nice things are nicer than the nasty ones." (140) This line of thought leads to the concept of luck announced in the title of the book:

> It was all very bad luck on Margaret and probably derived as he'd thought, before from the anterior bad luck of being sexually unattractive. Christine's more normal i.e. less workable, character no doubt resulted from having been lucky with her face and figure. But that was simply that. To write things down as luck wasn't the same as writing them off as non-existent or in some way beneath consideration. Christine was still nicer and prettier than Margaret, and all the deductions that could be drawn from that fact should be drawn; there was no end to the ways in which nice things are nicer than nasty ones. It had been luck, too, that had freed him from pity's adhesive plaster. (242-43)

The world of *Lucky Jim* is funny because it reflects all that is absurd in this world. Logic is not the guideline for reward and punishment. A fool like Ned Welch is a Professor and Head of the Department of History and his pampered son Bertrand, who is doing nothing to earn a living has the best life or has to offer, while an intelligent man like Jim Dixon exists in a state of uncertainty, weighed down by economic and social problems. Dixon is the embodiment of intelligence and basic goodness. Full of vitality and vibrating with life, he is the standard by which other characters in the novel are judged and evaluated. It is true that Jim is full of impish pranks making surreptitious telephone calls, swiping other people's taxi, defacing a portrait of the cover of a magazine and writing anonymous letters—but they are quite harmless and invariably directed against characters who deserve it. Jim cannot resist playing jokes, it is an extension of his personality.

Jim Dixon is from middle class and his sympathies are clearly with the downtrodden. He rises in righteous anger against the hypocrisy and phoney social plays that are threatening to disrupt the healthy values. Here he is the champion of orthodox morality. When judged against the Dixon measuring rod, the Welch family is right at the bottom closely followed by Margaret. Prof. Welch and Bertrand are mean, selfish, stupid and hypocrites, and Bertrand especially represents all that is base and vile in human beings. It is significant that they are represented as physically ugly. Amis believes that the face is the index of the soul—Welch has 'clay like' features and face like a 'Pig's Bum'; while Bertrand with his 'pointed beard, long ears, extra-ordinary eyes and baying voice' is a picture of the devil. They do not act or behave naturally and are forever enacting a role. Prof. Welch whose academic qualifications are suspected, plays the role of a scholar and whenever there is a threat of exposure he puts on mask of forgetfulness. Bertrand poses as an artist primarily because it enables him to lead a licentious life and court beautiful girls like Christine while hurling insults and abuses at non-entities like Jim Dixon. But when the mask is removed Bertrand appears to be morally bankrupt, ineffectual coward. He does not have the moral courage to love a pure, decent girl like Christine because he knows his worth—he is an adulterer. His affair with Carol Goldsmith and his promises to Christine prove him to be a two faced liar. He never intends to get serious with either of them. He uses Carol Goldsmith to satisfy his sexual desires and parades Christine as a status symbol and also nurses the selfish hope to procure a job through her, since he is incapable of finding one for himself. Yet the moment Christine gives evidence of her interest in Dixon, he rushes to Dixon and threatens him with dire consequences if he continued to meet his girl friend. Jim, on the other hand, stands in sharp and complete contrast with him. He is aware of the clandestine affair between Bertrand and Carol Goldsmith and yet never mentions a word about it to Christine.

He does however unsettle Bertrand, claiming full knowledge about his activities. A hopping mad Bertrand says: "If you ever tell this to Catherine I'll break your neck into so many . . . It's all right, I'm not the sort to do that Dixon said with a grin. I'm not like you. I can take Christine away from you without that, you Byronic taïl-chaser." (213) The ensuing fight and subsequent knockout of Bertrand is the symbolic victory of the values Dixon represents.

In the Margaret affair, too, Jim Dixon's basic goodness is revealed: "He'd been drawn into the Margaret business by a combination of virtues he hadn't known he possessed; politeness, friendly interest, ordinary concern, a good natured willingness to the imposed upon, a desire for unequivocal friendship." (10)

Margaret takes undue advantage of these qualities in Dixon's character. She is not only a hypocrite but also a bully and one who is capable of duplicity and like the Welches she, too, is unattractive. Dixon's dislike for Margaret becomes more pronounced as he gets an opportunity to contrast her to the beautiful Christine. Christine is vivacious, honest and fun loving as revealed in the sheet and blanket affair. When Dixon is in her company, he feels "like a special agent, a picaroon, a Chicago war-lord, a hidalgo, an oil baron, a Mohock." (115) She is the only character who rises to the level of Jim Dixon. Jim is speaking to Christine, the London girl who becomes his final reward. At this point in the novel, Christine is still connected with Bertrand Welch, the Professor's son and a pseudo artist. Christine and Jim are first beginning to recognize and acknowledge their feeling for each other when the following dialogue takes place:

> "If you can tell me whether you like greengages or not, you can tell me whether you're in love with Bertrand or not, if you want to tell me, that is."
>
> "You're still making it much too simple. All, I can really say is that I'm pretty sure I was in love with Bertrand a little while ago, and now I'm rather less sure. That up-and-down

business does not happen with greengages; that's the difference."

"Not with greengages, agreed. But what about rhubarb, eh? What about rhubarb? Ever since my mother stopped forcing me to eat it, rhubarb and I have been conducting a relationship that can swing between love and hatred every time we meet." (147)

Dixon stands up for middle class values but he is not biased against the upper class. When he confronts natural grace and goodness as in the person of Julius Gore Urquhart he is ready to appreciate it. What troubles him is that there is no systematic evaluation of one's moral worth. True, Jim is rewarded by winning Christine and getting a job more to his taste but as the title suggests the element of luck plays an important role in the case of Dixon. However, the fact that Dixon stands for orthodox morality and that he is finally rewarded confirms the view that Amis himself holds the human values sanctioned by tradition for sound and healthy living in the society.

However, some critics have apparently read many more moral meanings than is justified by it. For example, we can cite Robert Conquest's interpretation of *Lucky Jim* as a deeply religious novel. He visualizes Dixon as the representative of the human race and the faces he makes, too are given symbolical interpretations: "Dixon, the hero, is of course Everyman. In this capacity he is able to represent the whole human race (from Eskimo to Roman) and even to indicate the transcendental and universal scope of the Godhead by becoming briefly a Maritan. . . . But, and far more to our purpose, Dixon is also the Son of Man. The surname, with the cross at the centre for him to Di(c)on, is among the more overt conscious of the many signs the author has scattered."[18] He further attempts to bring out Christian symbols in the name of every character—Bertrand means 'bright raven,' i.e. Lucifer; Welch is really, Welt—ch, *Welt* is *world* in German and 'Ch' is the 'abbreviation of Church, in other words he is the anti-spiritual counterpart of true religion; Margaret is Marpelate and Michie is Michael.

The whole criticism of Robert Conquest seems to be motivated by a desire to emphasize the moral earnestness of the novel. However, it ends up with a systematic exaggeration of its moral intention which obscures the sturdy, robust, ordinary concern for common sense morality that Jim Dixon stands for. *Lucky Jim* on this reading appears to be some sort of an esoteric myth, a private pattern of symbols and allegories. This certainly is not the whole truth about the novel, even it is not a mere uproariously funny novel. To be sure, there is fun, abundance of comedy, but there is a central controlling moral impulse that derives its strength from the centre of traditional morality. It is plain and simple, it can be summed up by saying that good is rewarded and evil is punished. It is not only poetic justice, it is moral justice as well. Jim Dixon is morally just and is rewarded with a beautiful girl and a good job he likes. In this secular world these rewards are a pretty good measure of Dixon's moral worth.

Insofar as anything morally interesting is going on at all in *Lucky Jim,* it has to do with Dixon's decision to sever his relationship with Margaret Peel and run away with Christine Callaghan. Although Jim's scenes with Margaret allow her to let off a little psychological steam, they are on the whole rather tedious; as are Jim's reflections on his guilt, or unwillingness to accept his guilt over the way he has treated her. Whatever passably decent treatment Margaret had had from him, he supposes, was the result of a temporary victory of fear over irritation and pity over boredom. The irritation and boredom come over very well. It is the fear and the pity which remain mere words and rather too many of them. In any case, Dixon is let off the hook with Margaret when Catchpole, her previous lover, tells him the truth about the overdose of sleeping pills she took the night Dixon was expected to call at her flat. He warns him: "Don't try to help her [Margaret] any more; it's too dangerous for you. I know what I'm talking about. She does not need any help either, you know really. The best of luck to you, Good-bye." (243) A little later Jim Dixon comes to realize: "For the first time he really felt that it was no use trying to save those who fundamentally would rather not be saved. To get on trying would not merely be to yield to pity and sentimentality, but wrong and to pursue it to its conclusion, in húmane." (247)

In spite of the moral fuss Dixon makes about Margaret, his preference for Christine is really no more than a consequence of his frequently articulated conviction that nice things are nicer than nasty things, and that Christine's character is 'workable', while Margaret's is not. That does not seem like a very profound solution to Dixon's dilemma. He has simply substituted pragmatic for moral reasons for behaving as he does. The inconsequentiality of this form of moralizing by a character is demonstrated even more geographically in *Take a Girl Like You* when Standish subjects Sheila Torkington to an earnest, carefully considered, ever-so-closely reasoned lecture on why it would be wrong for him to enter into an affair with the seventeen-year-old daughter of his headmaster, and then goes on to say, "However, since you've taken the trouble to turn up" (278) and seduces her.

At the end of *Lucky Jim*, Dixon does not only get the girl, he gets the money too. More precisely, he gets the job in London as Julius Gore Urquhart's secretary. Bertrand Welch was also an applicant for the same job but he did not get it. Bertrand obviously does not deserve the job. He is a talentless person whom Dixon quite properly ridicules knowing him as Neddy Welch's son. But does Dixon deserve it? Gore Urquhart's opinion is that although he hasn't got the qualifications for the work, or any other work, he hasn't got the disqualifications either. What are the disqualifications Dixon hasn't got? But aren't knowing nothing about art, and not having a clue about how to make oneself socially acceptable to people rather massive disqualifications too, for the private secretary to a rich devotee of the art who intends to use him for "meeting people or telling people I can't meet them?" (238) This is not a real world of art and patronage, any more than the university was a real place where people taught things and learned things. It is a world in which farcical vitality and advanced powers of ridicule are rewarded by material success, as a gesture in the direction of comic justice. Just as the funnier the things are that John Lewis does in his effort to escape from Gruffyd Williams's house, the better time he deserves to have with Elizabeth on the beach, and the greater success he deserves to have at his interview with the library committee (later cancelled in favour of renewed marital harmony and a decent job with the coal board).

Another moral aspect *Lucky Jim* shares with many of Amis's later novels is the reappearance of dependence of the eighteenth century novels on rich benefactors, who are there to impress the hero with their admirable styles of life and often to provide him with a route to salvation through a lavish display of financial patronage. Gore Urquhart is the first of such figures in Amis's work—as free with his whisky bottle as he is with his sinecures. Gruffyd Williams plays the same role in *That Uncertain Feeling*. Although at first he seems a dull stick, later it transpires that he is a sensitive soul when Lewis and Elizabeth are victim of a car accident. He turns up again in a different guise in *Take a Girl Like You* as Julius Ormerod treads a delicate balance between the predatory sexuality and the decent respect for other people. Evidently, the stream of seemingly inexhaustible financial benevolence shamelessly admired in characters ranging from Fielding's Squire Allworthy (*Tom Jones*) to Dickens's John Jarndyce, has not seen damned up by the Welfare State. John Wain's Charles Lumley (*Hurry on Down)* also benefits from such liberal patronage, in his employment as Mr. Bracewright's chauffeur.

Lumley is a typical angry protagonist who rebels and then finds some niche for himself that fails to accommodate his former intention. The honesty of the intention becomes transformed into the useful reality. So are Dixon and Douglas Yandell, the narrator of *Girl* 20 (1971). But what Fredrick R. Karl calls "the expedience of reality" (229) has more in common with those merely literary rewards and punishments that eighteenth century and Dickensian heroes have handed out to them in the final chapters of the novels they belong to. Similarly, the protagonist of Kingsley Amis, Jim Dixon, with his arm around Christine, is able to say: "More than ever he felt secure; here he was, quite able to fulfill his role and as with other roles, the longer he played it the better chance you had of playing again. Doing what you wanted to do was the only training and the only preliminary needed for doing more of what you wanted to do." (149)

As Jim' s favourite role consists in doing what he wants to do and he is stumbling against the world he lives in. *Lucky Jim* ends in fantasy in an improbable justification of Jim's romanticized wishes.

III

That Uncertain Feeling was published one year after *Lucky Jim*. It was anticipated to be another knock about comic novel in the tradition of *Lucky Jim*. Amis surprised us by producing a work in which the moral theme is much stronger and the comedy more subdued. The good-humoured satire turns bitter as the lively Jim Dixon is replaced by a cynical John Lewis. However, the balance between comedy and morality is near perfection, as David Rees observes: "*That Uncertain Feeling*, distinctively combining as it does humour, social observation and an unequivocal attitude towards moral dilemma, is, I think, Amis's best novel to date."[19]

The relationship between the upper class and the middle class is the central theme of the novel and Amis is deeply concerned with the moral dimension of their relationship. The sanctity of marriage is contrasted to the illicit love affair between John Lewis and Elizabeth Gruffyd-Williams. These wealthy predators threaten the very institution of marriage, as their hunting ground is the economically poor middle class, whose people are lured by wealth to become gigolos at the risk of breaking their home. John Lewis loves his wife, yet he is tempted by the glamour of the Aberdarcy bourgeois. But the basic difference between John Lewis and Elizabeth is that whereas the former is aware of the moral values, the latter is not. The moral conflict begins when John Lewis starts violating traditional moral values and consequently feels guilty; Elizabeth does not experience such emotions. It is here that middle class morality scores over the upper class. John Lewis emerges from the experience cleansed with the realization that wealth is not necessarily elevating and poverty degrading. Lewis's decision to leave the town is the reaffirmation of traditional moral values centring in marriage. The conjugal relationship disturbed for the time being is restored. The temptation that had threatened to wreck his home life is overcome and a normal and sane relationship with his people is reestablished.

John Lewis is apparently happily married to Jean, whose beauty has begun to fade prematurely. The charm of their marriage is wearing off and John Lewis is going through a period of an uncertain kind of feeling in which he wants to do something but is not quite sure what. The feeling of unrest drives him into an affair with Elizabeth, the wife of Vernon Gruffyd Williams who is a member of the Aberdarcy Council, and Director of an oil company and obviously a rich man. The affair is doomed from the start primarily because they belong to two different classes. Lewis realizes this but is quite helpless against the charm of Elizabeth. His pumped up anger dissolves into thin air the moment she speaks to him. He is unaware that his growing involvement with this home-wrecker will lead to definite estrangement of relationship with his wife. He has reached a stage when he has begun to take his wife for granted. If ever he does something wrong all he has to do is to confess to his wife and everything will be all right. Jean comes to know about the affair between her husband and Elizabeth and she decides to give him a stern warning:

> Now you listen to me. Perhaps you think I don't know you. I do though. I know the look you get when you start fancying a woman. You had it that night at the party when you came over to me, thought you'd better not to spend any more time talking to her not with me there. I might spot you. . . . You think you can get rid of what you do by coming and telling me about it afterwards. Well, you can't. You know you'll always do what you want to do, why have you

> got a talk about it? Go off and do her if you want to, as long as you don't tell me. (160-61)

The warning ricochets not because Lewis is devoid of the finer feeling for his wife, in fact he has his private moral conflicts between right and wrong when he is not under the hypnotic spell of Elizabeth. He is well aware of his duties to his wife and he also knows that Elizabeth regards him merely as a pin-up boy. Yet he behaves like a man possessed, a puppet in the hands of Elizabeth, dancing to the tune she plays. One night Elizabeth drops him home alone, he finds his wife and children sleeping and a plateful of food waiting for him, he thinks: "As well as the private wash-day, tomorrow was inevitably going to be the time for holding a little private levee for guilt and anxiety and the rest of the old bunch." (94)

These moments of guilt decrease as the affair progresses. But no sooner is it consummated he decides to end it; realization dawns on him that all that Elizabeth stands for is mean and ugly, however attractive she may be physically. He goes home to discover that Jean in an act of vengeance has been sleeping with the despicable pervert. Their marriage is on the verge of collapse, but Lewis makes a determined bid to save it:

> Since I seemed to have piloted myself into the position of being immoral and moral at the same time the thing was to keep trying not to be immoral, and then to keep trying might turn into a habit. I was always at least until I reached the climacteric, going to get pulled two ways, and keeping the pull from going the wrong way or trying to, would have to take the place for me, of stability and consistency. Not giving up was the important thing. (239-40)

John Lewis constantly debates and worries about moral issues. Each time Elizabeth carries him off for the evening, he suffers pangs of guilt for deserting his wife for consorting with the Anglicized Upper Class. But he is never honest with Elizabeth. At one point he even intends to project his guilt by phoning her and telling her off, but after a long diatribe he notices that he has forgotten to press Button A; she hasn't heard a word he said. Clearly, this guilt is part posture, for John is singularly dense about moral issues. He does not understand Elizabeth and judges her by the rigid non-conformist code of his home village. When he maintains that he will give up the better job he gained through his affair with Elizabeth, he is unable to understand his wife's moral position. As he had already violated their marriage, he might just as well reap the benefits of the violation. John in the complex world of Aberdarcy can neither understand to follow a moral line of conduct nor live with the consequences of his own immorality. He is, therefore, unable to operate successfully in society. At the end, he only recognizes his own cowardly nature and retreats to the mining town he came from.

This is not only Lewis's resolution but also the message Amis conveys to us. The determined effort of John Lewis saves the marriage; they leave Aberdarcy and decide to settle in his native town of Fforestfawr, where he is employed as a clerk in a coal company. The job is not as good but the pay is not too bad. Jean thinks that this was a kind of running away but Lewis considered this running away 'a stroke of bloody genius', 'the important thing was not to give up', and he never gives up his effort to save his marriage. If it appears to be an escapist attitude everything is all right as long as a man abides by his principles. John Lewis is again exposed to temptation when a Professor's wife makes a pass at him. Lewis resists it. But will he be able to resist the next time and the time after that is the question we ask ourselves. The answer is 'yes', for Lewis's moral fibres have been strengthened and the fact that he did not succumb to the temptation this time bears evidence that he will not falter the next time.

The other lesson Amis drives home is that mixing with the upper class is futile and may be even dangerous and disastrous. Lewis learnt this lesson the hard way. His hope of getting the sub-librarian's job in the library he works in, is rendered possible with the chance acquaintance of Elizabeth whose husband is a powerful member of the Aberdarcy Council and the board that will be interviewing him. Time and again Elizabeth reminds him that jobs never come without lobbying and log rolling and that she would take up his case and do the necessary lobbying. For this favour John Lewis has to suffer the worst humiliations at the hand of the upper class. He is an intruder who has caught the fancy of Elizabeth and like all fancies, he too, will wear off. Therefore, Vernon Gryffyd-Wlliams thinks that the affair of Lewis with his wife poses no threat to him because her extra-marital affairs are well known to him and like her other lovers this 'librarian chap' too will fade out. He does, however, back him for the sub-librarian's job, not because he is particularly fond of John Lewis but because he will be able to spite Rowlands, the head librarian who does not like him. When Elizabeth lets slip this information just after he has made love to her, Lewis's humiliation is final and complete. He is merely a pawn in the hands of these power crazy people who are willing to play with his life according to their whim and fancy. Elizabeth's suspicion that Lewis is going through a mental conflict is confirmed when he asks her just how much had she to do with fixing the job. Her answer reveals that he would never have got the job on his own merit because nobody got jobs on his merit. A kind of remorse with complex feelings of guilt set in and Lewis tells Elizabeth:

> One of the things I feel rather strongly about is fiddles. You've no right to feel like that about a thing if you let fiddle go on when they're ones that happen to work in your favour. You can't just let yourself pack it in and not care. You're being a bastard if you do. And I've decided now I don't agree I could do the job better. (211)

The wrong he has done to his wife, the wrong he has done to Iuen Jenkins, perhaps a more deserving candidate who needed the extra money more than he did, and the wrong he has done against himself work on him simultaneously. A direct result is the immediate rejection of a hysterical Elizabeth who just cannot comprehend what has gone into Lewis. He sets about restoring his nearly ruined married life, wiping away all the humiliations he has suffered and emerging a morally rejuvenated man.

Amis's preoccupation with these vital moral issues reflects his growing concern at the degeneration of values in the modern society, where the orthodox moral values are held in a low premium and even the institution of marriage is threatened with the growth of free love. As a novel *That Uncertain Feeling* would have been better had Amis ended it after chapter sixteen with Lewis and Jean trying to find ways to mend their married life. The fact that Amis gives a definite solution at the risk of being called an escapist confirms how deeply traditional his own moral outlooks are. Referring to the moral streak running in the book, Anthony Powell says: "The fact that the second book pointed something of a moral cannot be held against him by those who grumbled about the anarchistic strain in *Lucky Jim*."[20]

Kingsley Amis in *That Uncertain Feeling* has given a glimpse of the upper class life which is led by Gruffyd-Williams. Their callous indifference to orthodox values is highlighted and their responsibility for its degenerative satirizing. Elizabeth is a serious menace to the well-being of the society of married couples. She is a predatory animal on the prowl from whom Lewis must run away to save his marriage. He meets another woman, then Professor's wife, a lesser menace to Lewis, because by that time Lewis has been taught a good lesson in sex morality. It is evident that Amis believes in the sanctity of marriage and dramatically shows its abiding moral authority.

The novelist is a creative artist who creates a world in his novels. Some of the characters are his spokesmen through whom he conveys his message to his readers. Jim Dixon (*Lucky Jim*) and John Lewis (*That Uncertain Feeling*) are instances of such spokesmen of Amis. The message Amis conveys through these two characters is that we must preserve the traditional (moral) values and dignity of human beings. We must also realize our responsibilities and perform our duties, and maintain a balance in all walks of life. Amis belongs to the middle class; therefore it is quite natural to have sympathy for the middle class and the downtrodden people. It may, therefore, be said that the preservation of human values and dignity, sympathetic attitude for the fellow beings, and the realization of guilt and to try to improve oneself accordingly are some of the aspects of the humanism of Kingsley Amis.

NOTES

1. James Gindin, "Kingsley Amis", D.L. Kirkpatrick, ed. *Contemporary Novelists*, IV edition, p. 29
2. James Gindin, *Postwar British Fiction: New Accents and Attitudes*, p. 41
3. Kingsley Amis, *Lucky Jim*, p. 238
4. Kingsley Amis, *Take a Girl Like You* (London:Victor Gollancz, 1960), pp. 221-22.
5. Fredrick R. Karl, *A Reader's Guide to the Contemporary English Novel*, p. 220
6. James Gindin, "Kingsley Amis," p. 29
7. Kingsley Amis, "My Kind of Comedy," *Twentieth Century*, July 1961, p. 47.
8. Kenneth Hamilton, "Kingsley Amis, Moralist," *Dalhousie Review*, Autumn 1964, p. 347
9. Kingsley Amis, "My Kind of Comedy," p. 50.
10. James Gindin, "Kingsley Amis," p. 29
11. *Ibid.*, p. 28
12. Kingsley Amis, *Take a Girl Like You*, pp. 159-60.
13. James Gindin, "Kingsley Amis," p. 29
14. *Ibid.*, p. 29
15. Kingsley Amis, *That Uncertain Feeling*, p. 47.
16. James Gindin, "Kingsley Amis," p. 29
17. *The Encyclopedia Britannica*, Vol. 8, University of Chicago, 1967, p. 752
18. Robert Conquest, "Christian Symbolism in *Lucky Jim*," *Critical Quarterly*, Spring, 1965, p. 88
19. David Rees, "That Petrine Cock," *The Spectator*, Vol. 215, No. 7157, August 1965, p. 268
20. Anthony Powell, "Kingsley's Heroes," *The Spectator*, Vol. 211, No. 29, 1963, pp. 709-10

CHAPTER VI

DORIS LESSING

Among young contemporary English novelists, Doris Lessing is intensely committed to active persuasion to reform society. She talks of the "sense of duty"[1] that makes her join organizations and defends her own support of Communism. Her sense of social responsibility leads her to search for her values and for the literary material among the working classes in London. Her commitment to a sense of social responsibility and a pursuit of those oppressed by society also infuses her fiction about colonial Africa which makes her theme humanistic. It clearly shows that Doris Lessing is one of those novelists who are ready to 'stand with the unfortunate.'

The series of the novels that deal with Martha Quest's growing up demonstrates a strong endorsement of the heroine who is anxious to change society "to work actively for a more humane and just world."[2] Martha encounters difficulty in attempting within the severely restrictive society of colonial Africa to define herself both personally and politically. In her quest for values, she joins the Communist Party early in World War II, but finds the Party unable to do anything about colonial Africa's principal problem—'the division between white and black."[3]

The African fiction of Doris Lessing shows her scorn for the half-hearted liberals and the aristocrats who do not really commit themselves to the downtrodden. In a short story entitled "A Home for the Highland Cattle" (1956) the newly arrived colonial woman is anxious to treat the native house boy with justice and humanity. She is even willing to steal her landlady's huge picture of prize highland cattle so that the houseboy can legitimize his mistress by buying her as a wife. The white woman tries to understand the way black society operates and the boy genuinely appreciates her efforts but still, at the end of the story, the white woman fails to recognize her former houseboy as she watches the police marching him off to jail. In another story "Little Tembi" (1956), a white woman's special fondness for a black boy whose life she once saved, turns the boy into a wheedling thief. The boy is unable to accept his position in the black society. His ambivalent position destroys him, while the kind-hearted white woman sits by wondering what has happened. Both these women ultimately betray those they tried to help. But Doris Lessing strongly endorses those who are more systematically committed to work for socially oppressed. Her intense feeling of political and social responsibility is carefully worked into specific historical situation, reflecting upon the essential human situations.

From 1952 to 1969, Doris Lessing published the five novels to make the series entitled *Children of Violence.*[4] Taking on the largest possible obligations that a novel of development might impose upon an author, she wished to dramatize "the individual conscience in its relations with the collective."[5] Her example of the individual conscience, Martha Quest has become a character whom we mentally lift from the page and incorporate into our own lives as a reference point.

A writer must speak for himself as well as for others. By doing so he serves as a voice for the voiceless, as a witness for the inarticulate, and helps to form a community of the like-minded people. He can reveal that what we thought a private hallucination is actually a collective thought, literature can grant us our sanity. Throughout *Children of Violence*, the picture of the four-gated city embodies harmony, reconciliation and integration. Her answer to Babel in which she speaks against a history that has alternated centrifugal desires to separate with centripetal desires to dominate. It has been her new Utopia, "rooted in the body as well as in the mind, in the unconscious as well as the conscious, in forests and deserts as well as in highways and buildings, in bed as well as the symposium."[6] It is concerned with the future toward which the individual conscience might aspire.

In this series, Martha grows up amid the distrust between English men and Afrikaners, and their common hatred of blacks. The tension of which she is aware from childhood becomes the major conflict she confronts in the adult world. Already refusing her mother's self-imposed constricted role, Martha drifts toward "socialism and atheism, becomes pro-black and attempts anything that will lead to substantial personal values."[7]

Doris Lessing has devoted a tetralogy to an African problem i.e. "the relationship of black and white, ruled and ruler."[8] Besides the colour, she is concerned with the rights of a woman in a world of man and "looks to the politics of the left-wing to bring justice to women and blacks alike."[9]

Her "free spirits"[10] no less than those of the Brontes or George Eliot have to love and be loved; this need creates the muddle that makes them human. No single segment abstracted from it is the business of the novelist. Jack tells Anna Wulf in the novel *The Golden Notebook* 1962):

> To humanism; he thinks and says: "the idea of humanism will change like everything else." I [Anna Wulf] say: "then it will become something else. But humanism stands for the whole person, the whole individual, striving to become as conscious and responsible about everything in the universe. But now you sit there, quite calmly, and as a humanist you say that due to the complexity of scientific achievements the human being must never expect to be whole, he must always be fragmented."[11]

The international crises of the second-third decades of this century have put many established ideas and values upside down. The two World Wars have left the world with huge debris and everlasting scars. Modern scientific achievements have added much fuel to the fire. It is an age of pollution and explosion. It is an age of disillusionment and frustration. It is an age of neurosis and perversion. Life is but an extension of boredom. A vicious sense of failure is lurking from above and from within. Fredrick R. Karl, referring to an interview given by Doris Lessing, makes the point sharply clear: "In a May 1969 interview at Stony Brook, New York, Doris Lessing spoke of the period in which *The Golden Notebook* takes place as a time when everything is cracking up. . . . It had been falling apart since the bomb was dropped on Hiroshima. Then, in a statement which carries the full force of the self-hatred and driven quality we sense in Anna-Ella, she says: 'Throughout my life I've had to support parties, causes, nations, and movements which stink.' She states further, 'I feel as if the Bomb has gone off inside myself and in people around me. That's what I mean by cracking up. It's as if the structure of the mind is being battered from inside. Some terrible thing is happening.'"[12]

It is not only Doris Lessing who has undergone such ordeal, but most of the novelists of her age have experienced such terrifying, disintegrating and killing ordeals. Durrell portrays Alexandria as a hell. Anthony Powell's novels are filled with mythical hells. Even her contemporary poets are not free from the perilous experience of life. Ted Hughes, in his famous poem *Cadenza: The New Poets* (1978), presents this state of mind:

> The Full, bared throat of a woman walking water,
> The loaded estuary of the dead,
> And I am the cargo
> Of a coffin attended by swallows,
> And I am the water
> Bearing the coffin that will not be silent.[13]

In this chaotic and confused world it seems that there is no hope. Adam has lost his Eden, Pandora's box is open, emitting all the vile, furious and ferocious objects. Social security and personal ease are threatened by a new dragon. Nothing is left charming and lovely. Lust of life brings more complexities. Death seems the only solution facing life in this mad, strife-torn world. Sylvia Plath wants to celebrate this desire of death. Rosenthal notes: "Under all the other motifs of Sylvia Plath's work, however, is the confusion of terror at death with fascination by it."[14]

Dramatists like Samuel Beckett and Harold Pinter watch a bleak and gloomy picture but give a message of hope, like a silver lining in a dark cloud. Their uncompromising rejection of an easy solution or cheap illusion of comfort ultimately has a liberating effect. The nature of man is such that in the very act of facing up to reality of his condition, his dignity is enhanced. He is defeated by a thing by which he is taken unawares.

All these writers, more or less, have their impact on Doris Lessing, but of all, she seems to be the most perceptive, analytical and thoroughly insighted as well as far-sighted novelist. Her journey from *Martha Quest* (1952) to *The Four-Gated City* (1969) is never a journey of Alice in Wonderland. It is a journey from hell to hell but the traveller is alert, conscious, struggling, losing, winning and crystallizing. We do not find such a vast panorama of life in any writer of her generation. She seems to attempt on cosmic writing. On the one hand there is the fading splendour of the setting sun of the Christianity and on the other hand, there is the temptation of Lawrentian sex. Between these two poles, Doris Lessing stands watching the devitalization of man and his reduction to a "nice piece of flesh."[15] William Shakespeare, in most of his tragedies, has used the imagery of animals and vile insects to show utter degradation of man. King Lear howls like a jackal and says:

> And my poor fool is hanged! No, no, no life!
> Why should a dog, a horse, a rat have life,
> And thou no breath at all? Thou wilt come
> No more,
> Never, never, never, never, never!
> Pray you undo this button. Thank you, Sir.
> Do you see this? Look on her. Look, her lips.
> Look there, look there I.[16]

Ella, one of the major characters of the novel *The Golden Notebook,* gradually develops, hatred against man. For her a man remains only "as a species of highly trained middle-class animal." (307-8) England is no more the right place for her. She thinks of her daughter Janet who "will grow up in England, a country full of men who are little boys and homosexuals and the half-homosexuals." (395) Her subconscious and unconscious layers of brain are full of terrible dreams of a green crocodile and a dwarfed malicious man. She writes:

> I slept lightly, with terrible dreams. The dream that kept recurring was myself with the old dwarfed malicious man. In my dream I even noticed a sort of recognition, so there you are, I knew you'd turn up some time: he had a great protruding penis sticking out through his clothes, it menaced me, was dangerous, because I knew the old man hated me and wanted to hurt me. (544)

D.H. Lawrence in *Sons and Lovers* (1913) has presented two female characters—Clara and Miriam, besides Paul's all-absorbing all-consuming mother. There Clara stands for 'all flesh' and Miriam for 'pure spirit.' Paul gets tired of both and returns to his mother. Man's incapability of satisfying a woman sexually has been emphasized with restraint in the novel but in *St. Mawr together with the Princess* (1925) Lawrence has exposed the male completely. The same animal imagery is pronounced to show Lou's concept of a perfect man. He is the animal-man of her dream. She tells her mother:

> We have no minds once we are tame, mother. Men are all women, knitting and crocheting words together. He stands where one can't get at him. And he burns with life. And where does his life come from, to him? That's the mystery. That great burning life in him, that never is dead. Most men have deadness in them, that frightens me so because of my deadness. Why can't men get their life straight like St. Mawr and then think? Why can't they think quick, mother: quick as a woman: only farther than we do? Why isn't men's thinking quick like fire, mother? Why is it so slow, so dead, so deadly dull?[17]

James Joyce and D.H. Lawrence stand apart from each other in dealing with the animal instincts. Sisley Huddleston contrasts them in the following manner: "Lawrence stands for acceptance, and Joyce for rejection. Lawrence would find lust and all natural things bad; Lawrence rails against those who would suppress human or even animal instincts, while Joyce rails against those who exhibit animal or even human instincts. . . . Joyce is the Puritan who is shocked by the libertine: Lawrence is the libertine who would shock the Puritan."[18]

Doris Lessing, like Joyce, successfully and brilliantly brings out the chaos, the confusion and the psychological tension of the modern life. She is even farther than Lawrence in treating the animal instincts wrapped with sexual intensity, lust and passion without any veil of chastity and purity. She is the boldest of all the contemporary fiction writers who lets her mouthpiece Anna Wulf, the central character of *The Golden Notebook,* herald an equality with man. In this connection, Bergonzi writes: "On the face of it Anna has achieved a degree of personal freedom that the new woman of Ibsen and Shaw could scarcely have dreamed of; she is as free as any man in all the major spheres of life, professional, intellectual and above all, sexual."[19]

Doris Lessing has focussed her attention on many points and problems. In Durrell's *Alexandria Quartet*, the action takes place in Alexandria which becomes a character. Lessing stretches her canvas from Rhodesia to Moscow and folds and unfolds it from London. She takes up fragments of War, Sex, Red Politics and women's Liberation and above all of the art and artist. She brings the fragmentations, compartmentations into a composite whole and calls it *The Golden Notebook.* Doris Lessing writes about her own experiences which went into making this huge book of six hundred and thirty eight pages:

> "Bound. Free. Good. Bad. Yes. No. Capitalism. Socialism. Sex. Love . . . " says Anna in Free Women, stating a theme—shouting it, announcing a motif with drums and fanfares . . . or so I imagined. . . . But no. Other themes went into the making of this book, which was a crucial

> time for me: thoughts and themes, I had been holding in my mind for years come together. (10)

Doris Lessing is a writer of radical opinions, but has never allowed herself to become a doctrinaire: her humanitarian sympathies embrace the whole sweep of the relation of the individual conscience to the collective. Her African books are concerned not so much with 'the colour problem' as with the human problem. Michael Thorpe says in his book entitled *Doris Lessing* (1973): "Her main business is with the white settlers she knows best; and her approach is often to contrast their natural and human imperfections with their position of political or technological advantage."[20] In respect of colour Doris Lessing says in *The Golden Notebook*:

> Then I [Anna Wulf] look and it is like a vision—time has gone and the whole history of man, the long story of mankind, is present in what I see now, and it is like a great soaring hymn of joy and triumph in which pain is a small lively counterpoint. And I look and see that the red areas are being invaded by the bright different colours of the other parts of the world. The colours are melting and flowing into each other, indescribably beautiful so that the world becomes whole, all one beautiful glittering colour, but a colour I have never seen in life. This is a moment of almost unbearable happiness, the happiness seems to swell up, so that everything suddenly bursts, explodes—I was suddenly standing in space, in silence. Beneath me was silence. (256)

Her search for a 'world ethic' does not end with the recognition that the Marxist 'dream' has turned into a nightmare. Unlike many disenchanted writers she has not compromised her artistic integrity in the service of a narrow creed. Here it would be better to compare the disillusionment of Doris Lessing with Communism to that of George Orwell and Ignazio Silone. Whatever the motives underlying the Spanish interlude may be, the fact remains that it marked the second crisis of George Orwell's adult life. Eventually, it revealed to him the hard facts about Communist politics. Little wonder, then, that *Homage to Catalonia* (1938) turns out to be a frankly written book about his disillusionment with Communism. Indeed this grim truth has been laid here with so much of moral concern that it may seem tempting to read the book as a confession.

Now at this point, one should remember that in the forties, it had becomes a usual experience to hear the story of some one's involvement and then of his disillusionment with Communism. Besides, most of the disillusioned people were as loud in declaiming Communism as they had been once in acclaiming it. However, things were different with Orwell. One thing that we can most confidently say in his case is that there was nothing negative or denigratory in his revulsion from Communism.

Now, for a close parallel, we may turn to Ignazio Silone who has given an account of how he broke with the Communist Party. Silone writes:

> It was a great crisis in my life . . . and one that, I suppose, has left scars. Although I tried to be an efficient Communist I was never a very good one, because I thought that Communist was something that it is not. It took me longer to find that out than it should have done, but all during that period one was so busy in the day-to-day activities and dangers of fighting for freedom that one had no time to scrutinize the true nature of Communism. When the confrontation with reality could no longer be delayed, it was even then, although 1 had no choice, very hard to leave the Party, to leave so many of my comrades, some of them dead, some of them in prison. Yet in a way, when the time came, I think the inner severance had already been made.[21]

But in her contribution "The Small Personal Voice" to *Declaration* (1957), Doris Lessing attacked critics for failing to see that the theme of *Children of Violence* was a study of the individual conscience in its relations with the collective. The Marxist word 'collective' should not mislead; the unity she seeks is older than any political dogma and is the goal of the questing artist, and not of the politician. She looks back in *Declaration* to the great realists, praising their 'humanity' and "love for people"[22]—Tolstoy, Balzac, Dostoevsky, Stendhal and Mann as the last of those whose work was capable of 'strengthening of a vision of a good which may defeat the evil'. It is significant that these names are all European; there is little precedent in English fiction for the kind of visionary sweep over society she aims at. Her positive claims for the novelist, on the face of it, modest in fact, asks as much of him as can be hoped. In an age of committee art, public art, people may begin to feel again a need for the small personal voice, and this provides confidence to writers and with confidence the knowledge which is needed for the warmth and humanity and love of people.

During her stay in South Africa, Doris Lessing gets herself acquainted with racial problems, social problems and supernatural beliefs of the Africans. She becomes an active member of the Communist Party with a view to getting social justice for the oppressed and equal rights for the women. But she is disillusioned very soon and resigns from the Communist Party. Her novels, from *The Grass is Singing* (1950) to *The Golden Notebook* and *The Four-Gated City*, are the records of the 'thoughts and themes which she has been holding in her mind for years': "Much of her work is on three themes: the necessity for active interest in political issues, the psychology of ageing women, and the conflicts of generations than their elders. *The Golden Notebook* is an ambitious and impressive attempt to illuminate these themes by repeating them with variations in a single book."[23]

The humanistic theme of Doris Leasing, based on her commitment to a sense of social responsibility, is found in all her novels but we discuss here this theme in her two novels *The Golden Notebook* and *The Four-Gated City*.

II

In *The Golden Notebook*, Doris Lessing presents Anna Wulf, the novelist writing a novel and keeping several notebooks revealing different layers of her life. The revitalization of the male of the human species, she finds, is partly due to the quest of women for freedom with the result that an inner bomb seems to have gone off shattering the human personality in the West. Like D.H. Lawrence, Doris Lessing is vitally interested in making life possible in the modern world. She is also seriously interested in art whose nature is discussed by Ella and Saul Green in detail in *The Golden Notebook.* She writes in the preface of the book: "But my major aim was to shape a book which would make its own comment a wordless statement to talk through the way it was shaped." (14)

The Golden Notebook is probably the most important single novel published in England since the War. Its theme is announced in the first line of the first section 'Free Women'. The two women, Anna and Molly, are alone together. "The point is," said Anna as her friend came back from the telephone "the point is that as far as I can see everything is cracking up." (3) The theme is developed in a number of materials. Within the 'Free Women' section it is dramatized above all in the behaviour of Tommy, Molly's son who deliberately becomes a psychotic.

At the same time in the 'Black Notebook' section the tension of mutual malice and self-contempt is found. But she also analyses her own inspiration in writing it. She says:

> The novel is about a colour problem. I said nothing in it that wasn't true. But the emotion it came out of was something frightening, the unhealthy, feverish illicit excitement of war time, a lying nostalgia, a longing for license, for freedom, for the jungle, for the formlessness . . . when I think back to that time. . . . I have to first switch something off in me, now writing about it, 1 have to switch it off, or a story would begin to emerge a novel and not the truth. (63-64)

The poignancy of this, for Anna Wulf as novelist or for Doris Lessing is of course the resistance it signals to write again. But it is important to her as political and moral being too. She continues:

> Nothing is more powerful than this nihilism, an angry readiness to throw everything overboard, a willingness, a longing to become part of dissolution. This emotion is one of the strongest reasons why wars continue, and the people who read Frontiers of War will have had fed in them this emotion, even though they were not conscious of it. That is why I am ashamed and why I feel continually as if I have committed a crime. (64)

The 'Red Notebook' describes about the splitting and splintering of political groups, and the counter play of truth and lie, moral enthusiasm and cynicism, each corrupting the other among Communists. When she rejoins the Party, she says in her first interview: "both pleased me—being back in the fold so to speak already entitled to the elaborate ironies and complicities of the initiative; and made me suddenly exhausted. I'd forgotten, of course having been out of the atmosphere so long, the tight, defensive, sarcastic atmosphere of the inner circles." (155)

The 'Yellow Notebook' reflects in fictional form—Anna's love affair with a man who is determined from the start not to commit himself to her and the strain this creates out of which she splits herself into psychic parts.

The 'Blue Notebook' describes Anna's sessions with Mrs. Marks, a Jungian psychoanalyst, who sees her cure exclusively in terms of her starting to write again—to resume her sacred vocation as artist while Anna is deeply ambivalent, deeply split about the value of art.

The 'Golden Notebook' is an attempt to combine the form of art and meaning with the raw, unfinished, tentative quality which she values. But from the point of view of the book's theme, the point of the 'Blue Notebook' sessions is that psychoanalysis fails as politics and eroticism, to heal the split and to prevent the crack-up.

The form of 'Free Women' is very Lawrentian. It is impossible to imagine that it could have begun the way it did if *Women in Love* (1921) had not begun this way. The doctrine of sexuality also is Lawrentian despite the connotation of free women. In the 'Yellow Notebook' we are told that Ella "floated darkly on her love for him, on her naivety which is another word for a spontaneous creative faith . . . what Ella lost during five years was the power to create naivety." (211-12) Indeed the 'Yellow Notebook' even decides that all her unhappiness derive from her trying to abandon conventional behaviour and trying to be 'free.' Anna and Molly talk of 'real women' and even 'real men' in a way that would shock a sexual libertine and the treatment of homosexuality is very hostile. Indeed, the relationship depicted in *The Golden Notebook* between Anna and Saul may be seen as a conflict and coming together of the Lawrentian mode of eroticism which is embodied in Anna

The book's ultimate message is spoken by Paul, one of the young men in the African group in the following manner:

> Comrade Willi, would you not say that there is some principle at work not yet admitted to your philosophy? Some principle of destruction? Willi said, in exactly the tone we had all expected: There is no need to look any further than the philosophy of the class struggle and as if he'd pressed a button, Jimmy, Paul and I burst out into one of the fits of irresponsible laughter that Willi never joined. (427-28)

Doris Lessing has an extraordinary barometric sensitivity to the social climate but she anticipates trends rather than capping them with a novel. Thus the encyclopedic study of intellectual, political women in *The Golden Notebook* preceded and in a sense introduced the Women's Liberation Movement. Despite her heroine Anna's insistence that she and her friend Molly are completely new types of women, there is an implicit continuity between their experiences, emotions, values and the great line of the independent artist women of the past.

The Golden Notebook is a monumental achievement of Doris Lessing in which she deals with twentieth century women and the female tradition. She believes that the people are heading for a global catastrophe through germ warfare, or breaking down of civilization. Sex and gender are irrelevant in terms of these human disasters. The change in Lessing's fiction from the individual to the collective, from personal to the communal, from female to the global consciousness seems at first like an abrupt transformation. It has however, been a systematic will and process of escape from a very painful encounter with the self, with the anguish of feminine fragmentation. The term feminine has class connotation for Lessing as well as suggestions of weakness, affectation and emotionality. The affliction of feminine sensibility portrayed in *The Golden Notebook* is a parody of a lady author, who notes in her journal how essential it is "to have clean linen on one's bed everyday." (438) In an interview that came out at the time the novel was published, Doris Lessing used similar language to describe Virginia Woolf:

> I've always felt this theme about Virginia Woolf—I find her too much of a lady. . . . I feel that her experience must have been too limited because there is always a point in her novels when I think fine, but look at what you have left out.[24]

In *The Golden Notebook* Anna finally convinces herself that the personal is political, if Marxism means anything it means that little about the emotions reflects "what's real since the emotions are a function and product of a society." (43)

Lessing's heroines systematically imply a semi-mystical theory of thought transference to avoid responsibility for their own sensations and their own feelings. When she breaks down in terror and self-loathing, Anna consoles herself with the thought that she is expressing someone else's anxiety state, "what I was experiencing was not my thought at all." (575) The experiences of Martha, Anna and Ella are the experiences of Doris Lessing herself transformed into art in *The Golden Notebook*. Martha has her first sexual affair with Adolf King whom she rejects later at the advice of Mrs. Stella. Her second man is Doggie who fucks her and at the end marries her. Finally Martha divorces Doggie and marries a German Communist only to find him suffering from sexual debility. She divorces him before coming over to London where she finds devitalized males and neurotic women everywhere. The characters in *The Golden Notebook* are 'boulder pushers.' Anna Wulf and Molly separate, kissing each other, Anna declares her intention to do the Marriage Welfare Work and Molly announces to marry again.

The search for identity is the crucial point in Lessing's novels. All the characters are desperately in search for identity. Soul Green says: "My God, what we've lost, what we've lost, what we've lost, how can we ever get back to it, how can we get back to it again." (605) Anna is afflicted "by the feeling of doom, fate, inevitability," (599) Saul shouts: "I am I, Saul Green, I am what I am, what I am." (565)

The Golden Notebook recalls other compendium of women's attitudes. It is in a different time and place than George Eliot's *Middlemarch* (1871-72). In that novel Dorothea Brooke is of course a less obviously sexual creature than Anna Ella of *The Golden Notebook*. But Dorothea's main actions do focus upon men as sexual object. After her marriage with Casaubon, Dorothea's later movement toward Will Ladislaw is a direct response to her continued virginity. It is an attempt to complete herself with a male. Without losing sight of the delicacy of Dorothea's emotional ballet, we may say that the undercurrents are strongly sexual and that intellectual satisfaction is impossible without physical completion. By hinting at the unmentionable—a woman's need for orgasm—and by advocating the very feelings normally held to be degrading *Middlemarch* as a liberating novel for women. Doris Lessing for her portraits has adopted indirectly the unlikely form of the descent into hell, a mythical pattern characterized by her female protagonists in their relationships with men. Like Persephone, her women emerge periodically from the underworld to tell us what went awry—and it is usually sex. If the Bomb exists out there in every Lessing novel, then within each woman who tries to transcend the traditional protection of housewife and mother, there exists a comparable bomb, which threatens to explode whenever she tries to live without men, or even when she lives with them.

The key issue of *The Golden Notebook* is human relationships, especially the relationships between men and women as a key image of modern humanity. Sexual liberation, from the female side and sexual restructuring from the male, is necessary. But in 1969, Doris Lessing says: "I'm impatient with people who emphasize sexual revolution, and go on with the important matters."[25]

Her turn upon herself is curious. For this conflict between collective politics and personal matters has been the crux of her work of the last two decades. Anna's psychiatrist, in fact, suggests that her political activity is an avoidance of personal blockage. The conflict is real. The incredibly difficult question of man-woman relationship becomes 'going to bed', and sexual liberation seems an act of conscious choice, whereas before the very question of liberation raised all the familiar problems of identity and will.

She aspires instead to meet the need for the more varied view of the human condition such as Tolstoy or Stendhal could only provide. *The Golden Notebook* is about this need and how hard it is in our time for the novelist to meet it. The action is a purgative process which may or may not fit Anna to convey "a vision of a good."[26]

If literature is concerned with the self, it is also concerned with the self-control; in the beginning Anna cannot write because she fears spreading her feelings of 'disgust and futility', but by the end she has learnt to live through her divided selves. We do not see Anna's predicament as separate from her society, its ideals and failures. But she reflects these frustrations and sterility of living like this, without a central philosophy; but forces like Martha to accept the fading of the Marxist 'dream' she seeks a new centre.

Her search is reflected in the book's unusual structure which despite its bulk is no Victorian 'baggy monster.' By means of the notebooks Anna divided herself into four to avoid facing up the chaos; on one the Blue she tries to be honest and this especially is in the end superseded by the Golden, 'all of me in one book.'

The notebooks punctuate instalments of a conventional novel entitled 'Free Women' in which Anna herself is a character, using experience in the Notebooks selectively. If literature is analyzed after the event, the Notebooks represent 'event', 'Free Women' the literature or fiction. If we read the Notebooks, then the novel in that order, we would see how Anna, the unblocked writer of 'Free Women,' is using her fragmented experiences recorded in the Notebooks. The African material of the 'Black Notebook' which she cannot use, though it describes some of her most deeply felt experience, disappears. At the centre of the 'Free Women' is Richard, Tommy, Marian triangle from which in the Notebooks, Anna appears excessively detached. The Notebooks are used in Anna's novel as a crucial factor behind Tommy's attempt to commit suicide. After blinding, Molly comments with tragic irony, 'he is all in one piece for the first time in his life.' The motif of suicide had already been approached by Ella in the 'Yellow Notebook,' but as fictional projection of her own despair; in placing the Notebooks as a power for evil in 'Free Women' Anna accepts the moral responsibility for them.

Previously in the 'Yellow Notebook' we have seen Anna trying to fictionalize her experience. Ella is neither interested in politics nor in all the Red Materials. Anna's albatross is cast off. Anna says to John Butte:

> It is a crystallization of the intellectual rottenness of the party that the cry of nineteenth century humanism, courage against odds, truth against lies, should be used now to defend the publication of a lousy lying book of Communist firm which will risk nothing at all by publishing it, not even a reputation for integrity. (297)

In this Notebook anticipations of themes occur which is converted as positive use in the Golden Notebook. Anna can tell Saul Green that they are both 'boulder-pushers' (596) and in doing so implicitly accepts for herself the attitude of Mathlong, the African Nationalist, described in the 'Blue Notebook'. He is the man who performs actions, plays roles that he believes to be necessary for the good of others, even while he preserves as ironic doubt about the results of his actions. This particular kind of detachment is something we need very badly at present time.

If we see 'Free Women' as representing Anna's positive reshaping of her experience, we are bound to ask how good a novel it is. It is doubtful whether this is a very useful question; we do not read it alone, but as a skeletal piece of fiction whose flesh in 'life' the Notebooks provide. *The Golden Notebook* may be judged as a whole whose aim is to explore the plight of the socially responsive and responsible writer in the phase of disorientation and alienation in which we live. The fact that it also explores in depth the dilemma of the 'Free Women', woman's most intimate experience is incidental though indispensable to this theme.

The protagonist of *The Golden Notebook* as artist is no remote being, but one who has an uncommon responsiveness to common experience. This is recorded with such fidelity that Anna Wulf's primary significance as artist is overlooked. If it is lost it is impossible to respond adequately to the novel's larger meaning. Anna Wulf says in the novel: "Very few people really care about freedom, about liberty, about the truth, very few. Very few people have guts the kind of guts on which a real democracy has to depend. Without people with that sort of guts a free society dies or cannot be born." (484)

III

The four gates to the four houses where Martha stays are themselves microcosms of English society. This society follows on the holocaust of the Second World War. Whereas gates are once entrances that one opens while seeking something or someone, they are now barriers which close off exits. The four bleak houses of England are: the restaurant at the beginning where Martha is known as Mattie and is expected to lose herself in a dull marriage. Second is the house of Mark Coldridge who is a writer and close to the centre of power. He is besieged by predatory journalists and the house is a centre of madness in activity, frustration as well as some kindness. Third is the house of Jack. Here girls go to become prostitutes where Jack sits like a spider and wants to catch them on their fly. Finally the house of Paul is found. Paul is Mark's nephew who is sexually crippled.

The connecting link among all the houses, all the gates, is Martha herself. At the opening of the novel she visits the restaurant when she arrives in Post-War London. She then seeks a job as a secretary, but accepts temporarily a post as Mark Coldridge's housekeeper. The house becomes a walled-in medieval fortress, which protects her against further action, even further thought and the job turns into a way of life. Using Mark's house as a base of operations, Martha occasionally ventures out to have casual sex with Jack and to continue the debasement of her former intentions.

The Four-Gated City chronicles the breakdown of decorum most completely and ends with Martha's search for documentation on the discoveries she has made by experimenting with her own psyche. Once she exercises her fears of seeming dotty and indecent which she finds in fantasy writing, in hermetic philosophy, in the quotations from Sufis that are taken out of the text and made into epigraphs: "Organs come into being as a result of a need for specific organs . . . . what ordinary people regard as sporadic and occasional bursts of telepathic and prophetic power are seen by the Sufi as nothing less than the first stirrings of these same organs."[27]

Doris Lessing calls on evolutionary theory not of the Victorians, but of the Sufis. In the *Children of Violence*, she uses epigraphs to inform us of her intentions. They are annotations and shorthand exegeses. Significantly she begins part IV of *The Four-Gated City*, the last pillar in her blue print of the architecture of Martha's soul with passages about Sufi thought:

> Sufis believe that expressed in one way, humanity is evolving towards a certain destiny. We are all taking part in that evaluation. Organs come into being as a result of a need for specific organs. The human being's organism is

> producing a new complex of organ in response to such a need . . . so essential is this more rarefied evolution that our future depends upon it.[28]

Both tropes and theory reinforce the sense that growth has the force of natural law. It transcends individual choice. We may choose to obey or to neglect that law to dwell within its imperatives or to deny them, but we cannot decide whether or not it exists.

Doris Lessing's commitment to the expansion of consciousness tempts one to call *Children of Violence* "the adventure of interiority; the story of the soul that goes to find itself that seeks adventures in order to be proved and tasted by them to find its own essence."[29] She herself has named *The Four-Gated City* a Bildungsroman: "This book is what the Germans call a Bildungsroman. We don't have a word for it. This kind of novel has been out of fashion for some time. This does not mean that there is anything wrong with this kind of novel." (655)

Doris Lessing modifies the Bildungsroman through a self-conscious interest in such larger political issue as "racism, class conflict and War."[30]Dagmar Barnow says that *The Four-Gated City* becomes a collective Bildungsroman which has its protagonists like Mark, Lynda and Martha. She cannot find the first volume a Bildungsroman in the strict sense of the word for: "Mattie is neither moving toward a choice, a determining decision she will make at one time or the other, nor is the fact that she is incapable of such a choice integrated into the substance and the structure of her developments."[31] Mattie moves towards the choice of leaving Africa and her general difficulty of the will is one of the novelist's deep interests.

Despite her liberal belief in the individual and freedom, Doris Lessing writes a Bildungsroman that goes beyond the picture of the atomistic self-spinning along a top social space. If Martha rejects the nuclear family, she enters an extended family in which cords of choice replace those of blood and law. If she refuses biological mothering she becomes a surrogate parent.

Lessing is too flexible to feminize wholly the nurturing role and evoke the spirit of a great mother to rationalize women as mothers.

For Martha, the political party, like the extended family, becomes a community of choice. Deftly, incisively, dryly, Lessing dramatizes the mechanics of the small progressive party: the lobbying, manouvering of agenda, interplay between insiders and outsiders. The desire for a charismatic leader is the gratifying sense of business, the feeding on ideology and hope because of the absence of real power. However, Martha is unable to find a party that fuses a ridicule ideology and power, vision and efficiency, prophetic zeal and historical wisdom, humanitarian ideas and human behaviour.

Doris Lessing is obviously reconciled to the comic promise of the Bildungsroman, that we can within history pass from youth to a semblance of maturity. She does so through the Sufi belief in "the possibility of a conscious evolution . . . this more rarefied evolution that our future depends on." (485) If each of us nurtures consciousness as we pass from youth to a semblance of maturity, if we join with others who are doing the same thing, then we may either avert the revelation or live through it and protect those children whose minds are even more potent than our own. Lessing adopts the myth of individual and collective rebirth. Such myths have consistently attracted her. In 1957, she exulted: "I'm convinced that we all stand at an open door and that there is a new man about to be born who has never been twisted by drudgery."[32] *Children of Violence* tests and retests these myths to retain them in a grimmer more shadowed form. In *Landlocked*, Thomas, naked in bed with Martha, says: "Perhaps there'll be a new mutation though. Perhaps that's why we are all so sick. Something new is trying to get born through our sick skins. I tell you, Martha, if I see a sane person, then I know he's mad. You know, the householders, it's we who are nearest to being—-What's needed."[33]

The theme of relationship between men and women of Doris Lessing is the same as that of George Bernard Shaw. No problem of modern society has exercised Shaw's imagination so powerfully as the problems of family, love, marriage and sex relations between men and women. Shaw objects to marriage and family because these institutions are based on false economics and false biology. As a biologist, he thinks that procreation is the most sacred work of all and as a socialist he demands that all works should be suitably paid for. Underpayment in the industrial world leads to *Mrs. Warren's Profession* (1898), but exploitation of women within the family is even a worst form of prostitution. The institution of family rests on a foundation of fraud. The husband thinks that he provides security, defence, livelihood, honour and prestige to the wife. But in reality, we are shown in *Candida* (1898), it is the wife who provides comforts for the man and keeps out vulgar cares from him. In *Back to Methuselah* (1921), he gives us glimpses of an ideal society in which Family and Marriage and private property are no more and the state is responsible for the rearing of the children. According to our codes of morality, a society of women who specialize in the breeding of children but do not recognize their own children is certainly scandalous, but then Zoo belongs to a society in which there are no scandals.

George Bernard Shaw is in favour of social and economic justice to women but he is against the worship and adoration of women. In the preface of *Man and Superman* (1903), he speaks contemptuously of the romantic adoration of women. Women are not incarnation of music, poetry and painting but they are flesh and blood as men are. The female for him is not the weaker sex, but the stronger sex in the sense that women's instincts are more compelling, their wills more determined and their sense of reality more vivid. A woman is not the pursued, but the pursuer; it is man who is wooed and won.

But on the other hand, D.H. Lawrence is of the view that physical union with the other sex is essential for integrated personal development, but he stresses the separateness of man and woman in union. There must be two in one, always two in one, an equilibrium, a pure balance of two single beings as the star balance in each other. The separateness in union is often stressed by the use of the dance symbol. Relationship of the sexes must be reconciliation of the opposites and not a domination of one by the other. For example, Birkin and Ursula in *Women in Love* (1921) achieve sexual harmony, because there is no attempt at domination but a recognition of otherness. For this purpose, D.H. Lawrence lays down the law of reconciliation of the opposites for self-fulfillment. Antithesis or the balancing of the opposites is the law of nature—night with day, light with darkness, the sun with the moon and the male with the female. Man is the sun and woman is the moon and the two must balance each other for their mutual fulfillment. However, a satisfactory adjustment can be achieved only when men and women recognize the essential otherness of each other. Without such recognition there can be no satisfactory polarization which the male and the female are by their very nature. There should be no attempt at domination, no over-possessiveness, no desire to suck the soul of others.

In one of the many scenes in which Doris Lessing insists that privileged moments of vision occur in our daily life, in our walks down an ordinary street, Martha broods:

> There was something in the human mind that separated and divided. She sat looking at the soup in front of her thinking . . . for the insight of knowledge she now held of the nature of separation, of division, was clear and keen—she understood . . . how beings could be separated so absolutely by a light difference in the texture of their living that they could not talk to each other, must be awry, or enemies. (82)

As Martha educates herself in sheer orgasmic pleasure, she experiences both a new simplicity of will, a clarity of action and a dissolution of the ego that serves, paradoxically, to strengthen that simplicity of will. As the boundaries of the self blur into the other, Thomas and Martha become each other's histories. Later with Mark and Jack, Martha finds in sex an even more expansive fusion between self and world, an access to "an impersonal current . . . the impersonal sea." Sadly Martha's most vital sexual experiences are with men who are flawed prophets: Thomas cannot pass beyond violence and chaos. Jack transmogrifies his knowledge of the body into sadistic domination. Mark, despite his brains and strength and kindness, cannot transcend Western rationalism. In his camp, after the Catastrophe, he writes: "I cannot stand that nasty mixture of irony and St. John of the Cross and the *Arabian Nights* that they all [Lynda, Martha, Francis] went in for." (652)

Martha's most educational prophetic experiences with a woman are sexual. Laying bare Martha's sexual growth, Doris Lessing balances delicate insight. Both maternal and exotic sexuality can threaten freedom. The woman in love is unappeasable, hungry, restless, and dependent upon her man. For Martha such lapses from liberation are characterization of a 'female self,' a simplistic genderizing of identity that Doris Lessing is most guilty of when she talks about female sexuality. Martha begins to practice a willed repression and indifference to sexual claims to avoid the constrictions of the 'female self' and to sharpen her capacity for insights. She has only one biological child. Later in London, she decides:

> When a woman has reached that point when she allies part of herself with the man who will feed that poor craving bitch in every woman, then enough it's time to move on.
>
> When it's a question of survival, sex the uncontrollable can be controlled. (301)

As Martha's powers enable her to lose the ego but not the world to shatter barriers but not to slump into violence, nihilism or infantile regression, she becomes a member of another community: that of her fellow sensitives. She first enters it with Lynda:

> One night, going down to see if Lynda was all right before she herself went to bed, she asked: "Lynda do you ever overhear what people are thinking?"
>
> Lynda turned swift delighted: "Oh," she exclaimed, "you do? I was waiting for you to . . . " (371)

Such a society, more than an esoteric cult, is the basis for politics of mind. As a party, it transcends hardened theories and harsh practices. As an organization, it abolishes tricks, manoeuvers, bureaucracies and tyranny. It emerges the virtues of anarchy and community. Francis exults when he becomes sensitive oscillating between optimism and rage:

> The old right of the individual human conscience which must know better than any authority, secular or religious, had been restored, but on a higher level, and in a new form which was untouchable by any legal formulas. We quoted to each other Blake's 'What now exists was once only imagined'—and did not for once, choose to remember the dark side of human imagination. (623)

It would be well to quote here an interview of Doris Lessing where she spoke of *The Four-Gated City* as a prophetic novel: "I think that the iron heel is going to come down. I believe the future is going to be cataclysmic." Further she says: "There is a new man about to be born . . . a man whose strength will not be gauged by the values of the mystique of suffering."[34] Till then it is gloomy: "The holocausts of the flesh in our life time have made it hard to believe that there can be any conversation between the shape of a face and the spirit." (709)

In *The Four-Gated City*, Martha and Lynda are mad only because they can tune into other people's thoughts. Leasing herself in a recent interview has disclaimed anything Unique or personal in her ideas and perceptions: "I don't believe any more that I have a thought. There is a thought around."[35]

Our discussion of the novels of Doris Lessing specifically *The Golden Notebook* and *The Four-Gated City* shows that she is a humanist who supports the cause of the downtrodden in the society. Women have been subject to suppression and suffering through ages, they were denied freedom and equal rights. Similarly the 'blacks' in Africa were treated as slaves by the 'whites' who were the rulers; the 'blacks' were also denied freedom and political as well as social rights. Doris Lessing champions the cause of women and the 'blacks' in her writings. Anna Wulf (*The Golden Notebook*) and Martha (*The Four-Gated City*) have been depicted as the spokesman of Doris Lessing who give a vent to the ideas and experiences of the author. They always involve themselves for the betterment of the fellow beings of their community. Particularly Anna Wulf thinks that women are equal to men, and is very conscious in giving proper justice to women. When she talks about women she does not talk about herself but she becomes the voice of the voiceless, a champion of women's freedom and rights. Martha is also involved in doing good for others. She is an optimist. She sees a bright future if people help and cooperate with each other and have fellow feeling and sympathetic attitude.

Doris Lessing is much worried about providing the 'blacks' with justice. She believes that the Communist Party will support and work for the cause of the 'blacks'; therefore she joins and becomes an active member of the Party. Her two mouthpieces—Anna and Martha—always involve themselves for the cause of the 'blacks' and demand that the 'blacks' must be given proper treatment, equal rights and justice as those of the 'whites'. Thus we find that the novels of Doris Lessing deal with the human problems, and they clearly reflect her fellow feeling, her optimistic outlook, and above all she raises her voice for the two downtrodden classes: women and the 'blacks.'

NOTES

1. James Gindin, *Postwar British Fiction: New Accents and Attitudes*, p. 65.
2. *Ibid.*, p. 68.
3. *Ibid.*, p. 69.
4. This series of novels contains *Martha Quest* (1952), *A Proper Marriage* (1954), *A Ripple from the Storm* (1958), *Landlocked* (1965) and *The Four-Gated City* (1969).
5. Paul Schlueter, *A Small Personal Voice: Essays, Reviews, Interview* (New York: Knopf, 1974), p. 14
6. Northrop Frye, *Utopia and Utopian Thought* (Boston: Houghton Mifflin, 1966), pp. 48-49.

7. Fredrick R. Karl, *A Reader's Guide to the Contemporary English Novel*, p. 303.
8. Anthony Burgess, *The Novel Now* (London: Faber and Faber, 1967), p. 99.
9. *Loc. cit.*
10. Michael Thorpe, *Doris Lessing* (London: Longman, 1973), p. 29.
11. Doris Lessing, *The Golden Notebook* (London: Michael Joseph, 1962), pp. 307-8.
12. Fredrick R. Karl, p. 292.
13. Ted Hughes, *Cadenza: The New Poets* (New York, O.U.P., 1978), p. 233.
14. *Ibid.*, p. 88.
15. *The Golden Notebook*, p. 201.
16. Peter Alexander, ed., *King Lear* in *William Shakespeare: The Complete Works*, The English Language Book Society and Collins (London and Glasgow, 1964), Act V, Scene III, Verses 304-10, p. 1112.
17. D.H. Lawrence, *St. Mawr together with the Princess* (London: Heinemann, Octopus Books, 1976), p. 245.
18. Sisley Huddleston, *James Joyce*, The Critical Heritage Series, Vol. II, pp. 549-50.
19. Bernard Bergonzi, *The Situation of the Novel* (London: Macmillan, 1970), p. 237.
20. Michael Thorpe, p. 2.
21. Kenneth Allosp, "Ignazio Silone," *Encounter*, March 1962, p. 49.
22. Michael Thorpe, p. 8.
23. David Daiches, ed., *The Penguin Companion to Literature*, p. 313.
24. Nancy Joyner, "The Underside of the Butterfly: Lessing's Debt to Woolf," *Journal of Narrative Technique*, V, 1974, pp. 204-5.
25. Fredrick R. Karl, p. 309.
26. Michael Thorpe, p. 25.
27. Idries Shah, *The Way of the Sufi* (London: Jonathan Cape, 1968).
28. Doris Lessing, *The Four-Gated City* (London: MacGibbon and Kee, 1969), p. 448.
29. Lucas George, *The Theory of the Novel: A Historico-Philosophical Essay on the Forms of Great Epic Literature* (1920), translated by Anna Bostock (Cambridge: M.I.T. Press, 1971), p. 89.
30. R. Catherine Stimpson, "Doris Lessing and Parables of Growth," Elizabeth Abel and Elizabeth Langland, ed., *The Voyage in Fictions of Female Development* (London: University Press of New England, 1983), p. 341.
31. *Loc. cit.*
32. Fredrick R. Karl, p. 301.
33. Doris Lessing, *Landlocked* (London: MacGibbon and Kee, 1965), p. 116.
34. Fredrick R. Karl, p. 310.
35. *Ibid.*, p. 301.
36. Raskin, "Lessing at Stony Brook", 1969, p. 173.

CHAPTER VII

ANGUS WILSON

Angus Wilson believes neither in., Christianity nor in "personal relationships and the private life."[1] His protagonists like those of Graham Greene are often placed in strange moral dilemmas. In Graham Greene's novels, however, man "works out his salvation through sin."[2] In Wilson's novels man works out his salvation through suffering.

The torment of human frustration, whatever its immediate cause shows that the self is imprisoned. Angus Wilson in his novels creates in memorable form the truth of such sufferings. He believes that every act of creation is a form of release. Critics like J.L. Halio, A.O. Cockshut and C.B. Cox feel that humanism is "a theme presenting all of Wilson's novels."[3] K.W. Grandson finds "Wilson's work valuable as social documentary."[4] K.W. Grandson, like C.B. Cox, argues that Angus Wilson represents the liberal humanist tradition. According to him "Wilson argues that liberal humanists tend to fight their battles inside their own consciousness rather than against the real evil in the outer world."[5]

According to Jim Hunter, Angus Wilson is not only a satirist but also "a full scale novelist, showing specially in his later works very human sympathies."[6] In his study of the novels of Angus Wilson, Valery A. Shaw says that the main difficulty of finding a suitable form for the expression of his liberal humanism becomes the perennial humanist dilemma—a world where the line between the moral commitment and social posturing is often thin and difficult to discern. Is there any way of living to which one can give clear assent? Wilson's answer is again a muted one; like Forster before him, he insists that in life and art alike, we must temper passion with intelligence and imagination with self-security.

Society is for Angus Wilson what a church might have been for a writer in the Middle Ages. Like E.M. Forster, he is an agnostic humanist. His novels have relevance not merely to the modern situation but always to the human predicament. Angus Wilson's novels deal with the condition of human soul which always tries to win new frontiers of consciousness. His memorable characters are generally humanist who struggle against the anti-humanist forces of the society including their own illusion and lust. Angus Wilson, in fact, belongs to the tradition of "liberal humanism."[7]

The hero of Angus Wilson's first novel *Hemlock and After* (1952) is a writer—Bernard Sands. Angus Wilson suggests that he wants to inhabit Sands's experience including his writing in a realistic way. The essence of this experience is a vision of aimless evil which undercuts the ameliorism of Sands's traditional humanist position. Sands is like George Eliot and Angus Wilson, a person who controls an acid wit and a natural cruelty in the interests of justice. Mrs. Curry is the opponent of Sands who is predatory and powerful. Both characters are good and centrally "realist"[8] in morals.

Angus Wilson's first three novels *Hemlock and after, Anglo Saxon Attitudes* (1956) and *The Middle Age of Mrs. Eliot* (1958) are regarded as his typical works in their precise registration of social nuance and the nature of their moral preoccupation. We dwell on responsibility and guilt in these novels. The tension is between the public life of busy achievement and the private life of spiritual cultivation. In Wilson's world, moral progress lies in the steady eradication of self-deception. Such preoccupations are, of course, part of central tradition of the English novel, the line of Jane Austen, George Eliot and E.M. Forster. It must be confessed that Angus Wilson's concern with these questions is at times a little finely drawn. It is not altogether easy to identify with the problems of the self-flagellating homosexual novelist, Bernard Sands in *Hemlock and After* or the spirituality sluggish historian, Gerald Middleton in *Anglo Saxon Attitudes.* In *The*

Middle Age of Mrs. Eliot, Meg Eliot, an archetypal liberal heroine, is good looking, sensitive and intelligent. Her husband is killed in an outbreak of casual political violence in an airport, the rest of the novel shows her brave attempt to make something of her life in widowhood and poverty.

The preoccupation with other people is declared immediately in the first sentence of the novel *The Middle Age of Mrs. Eliot.* Meg Eliot was well aware that in taking her place as the chairman of the committee for the third time in succession, she was acting in an "unconstitutional way."[9] Again we find later on the same page Meg having a sense of guilt: "Meg Eliot felt a bit ashamed when she considered how she had persuaded them."[10]

In the same way the dilemmas of his main characters are often connected with their relations to other people. He "attempts to portray"[11] Bernard Sands, the writer hero of *Hemlock and After* as a humanist. Two factors are responsible for shattering his inner complacency. These are,, as Colin Wilson observes, "his development of homosexual tendencies and his obsession that he feels a sadist pressure on seeing a male prostitute arrest in Leicester Square."[12]

Like the protagonists of Sartre and Camus, salvation does not worry him at all. What worries him is that his relation to society does not come up to his expectation. Consequently, he suffers from a sense of guilt which is responsible for meeting his end, the tragic end is not there in *Anglo Saxon Attitudes.* The central, character is a historian. His personal life is far from satisfactory. This is because of his moral cowardice. He has all the doubt that a historical discovery in which he participated is actually a fraud. He is successful in improving his "personal relations."[13] He wants historical world to know that the discovery was a fraud. What is striking to note is that his "inner life"[14] is good. This is because his personal relations are sound as they are established on a more satisfactory basis. Over and above, an adjustment has been possible as regards his relation to the society. Now he is in a position to enjoy a holiday in the "realm of fancy"[15] with a light heart.

In the first three novels, Angus Wilson's sense of nightmare appears in isolated incidents and recurring images but in *The Old Men at the Zoo* (1961) it moves into the centre of the action. This work is unique in Wilson's oeuvre in being as much a fable as a work of realistic fiction. His hero Simon Carter, secretary of the London Zoo, who is both an animal lover and an efficient administrator, tries to carry on with his work as best as he can. In doing so he embodies the classical dilemma of the public servant in a period of defeat and oppression. *The Old Man at the Zoo* is a bizarre and often violent narrative that seems to have enabled Wilson to face and to subdue his own fantasies.

His next novel *Late Call* (1964) is a work of relative serenity. We find in it the "infallible sense of his social fact."[16] *Late Call* explores the spiritual desolation of life in a New Town in the English midlands, where the gimmickry of affluence has become a way of life rather than an aid to living. Wilson employs the consciousness of Sylvia Calvert, a woman in her sixties, who has retired after a lifetime of managing small hotels. She is accompanied by her husband, who cares only for playing cards and reliving his days as a temporary officer in the First World War. She goes to live with her widower son Harold who is a progressive headmaster in the New Town of Carshall. He welcomes his parents to his fine modern house with a great display of filial feelings. But why and how they cannot live with Harold and his three teenage daughters is the story that Wilson goes on to tell with considerable insight and sensitivity. Sylvia is one of his most successful fictional creations. She is not at all an educated woman, but she has much native shrewdness and Wilson uses her honest but often baffled responses to make a remarkably sharp exposure of contemporary progressive attitudes.

In his latest novel *Setting the World on Fire* (1980), Angus Wilson dramatizes the conflicting forces of spiritual inspiration and rationality, individualism and society, disorder and order. Wilson expresses the tensions generated between these forces through his use of the myth of Phaethon, Tothill House and the double protagonists Piers and Tom Mosson. Each of them presents principally one of these polar forces while being appreciative of the roles of the other.

Angus Wilson carries on the humanist tradition among contemporary novelists in England. In a series of novels beginning with *Hemlock and After*, Wilson has shown an accurate understanding of English society and a sympathetic sense of the problems of the modern humanist. Bernard Sands, the hero of *Hemlock and After* is a successful writer and self-declared humanist. His message is that one should live according to one's nature. But he is helpless when he is aware of his own corruption. His wife Ella's attempts to carry on for Bernard have various results. But the Epilogue insists on the value of what Bernard had achieved in human terms. It is something that survives after the hemlock to influence the behaviour of those who had known him.

The distinction between doing and being is perhaps Ella's rather than Wilson's; at least, a kind of being which is justified by its influence on other people comes very close to doing. It is seen in another way that what must be sought for its own sake by the individual becomes for others a source of inspiration.

The theme of liberal humanism is found in all the novels of Angus Wilson but we shall discuss this theme in his two novels entitled *The Middle Age of Mrs. Eliot* and *The Old Men at the Zoo.*

II

Angus Wilson's most considered attempt to render the real world, to show a human being whole and in the round is *The Middle Age of Mrs. Eliot.* The rival—one can scarcely say the model—he sets himself against here is George Eliot. It is made explicit during the course of the novel that Wilson is attempting a heroine of a distinct type, one that has engaged the talents of some of our greatest novelists. In her various incarnations she has been Jane Austen's Emma, George Eliot's Maggie Tulliver and Dorothea Brooke, Meredith's Clara Middleton and Henry James's Isabel Archer. The very loftiness of her view of herself means that she lives at first in a state of self-delusion and her progress is the painful one of discovering the real nature of life and of herself. As we first meet her, apparently she is a highly successful wife of a successful barrister. She is beautiful and devoted in the most practical way to good works. She lacks only a child to have achieved fulfillment in her life. She is perhaps a little too pleased with herself, a trifle smug. It is all shattered when her husband is killed by a stray bullet in political assassination and she finds herself suddenly as a poor widow, face to face with the test of reality.

The Middle Age of Mrs. Eliot is concerned primarily with Mrs. Eliot's response to the sudden death of her barrister husband who leaves her at forty three, childless and with little money to make her way on her own inner resources. Meg Eliot is a smart, attractive woman who finds herself without her husband and her previous position. Her former life vanishes with death of her husband. She must salvage what she can without depending on others. The problem of the novel is to show how a woman who had rarely relied on herself before must suddenly survive through her own devices. At first her decisions result in a series of near disastrous setbacks. She meets successive defeats, whereas previously she had been successful. The road back is long, even longer for to find Meg Eliot attractive both as a popular matron and as a woman trying to regain self-confidence. Her former position as a society matron deeply in love with her ambitious husband. It does not augur well for her new situation in which she must perform heroically. However, the chief complement to Meg is her brother, David, whose life while different from hers, is equally uninteresting.

While Wilson catches quite effectively the life of a lonely widow as he drifts from one dingy place to the next. The centre of the novel is the woman herself and even though Wilson's regard for her struggle is affectionate and sympathetic. His feelings for the nightmarish quality of her life are evident.

The central character of the novel is an intelligent and well-read woman. On an aeroplane journey she has re-read *The Mill on the Floss* (1860) of George Eliot while her husband reads

Henry James's *The Portrait of a Lady* (1881). Meg Eliot associates herself with the heroines of these humanistic novels: "Isabel Archer and Maggie Archer face down on the table, and in the rock above, among the coats and suitcases. Emma and Lily Dale—all those girls were her, only that, born in a later century, she had avoided their defects; but their high spirits and their high hopes were exactly hers." (81)

In Meg's confidence that she had avoided their defeats is a note of a complacency which is destroyed very soon when Bill is shot intervening in an attempt to assassinate a minister. Meg Eliot is a woman of courage and resources. She fights to retain her sense of what her marriage has meant without seeking "to find him in sweet, cheating beliefs of after life, in all the pitiful round of some widow's church-going or medium frequenting." (107) The consolation of the elderly American Christian Scientist, Mrs. Fairclough that "they are not lost, they are only gone before," is meaningless that "truth is real and eternal, matter is unreal and temporal." (124) It is the greed with which she is devouring the homemade cakes, fruits and sandwiches. But there is no contempt in Meg and she is moved to pity when she sees the matchstick-thin legs on which the old lady moves away from her. Meg is never totally self-involved, and this makes her recovery possible.

It is however, a difficult process. She learns that high-handed charm with which she has carried things off before the death of her husband is ineffective in her reduced circumstances. She eventually quarrels with each of her three friends whose lack of money at first seems to suggest a possible deeper relationship. She takes a secretarial course to equip her for a job. But she falls ill before she can find one, and in convalescence she is taken to her brother's garden nurseries, Andreadaswood in Sussex.

David Parker, Meg's brother, is the second major character in the novel. He is a pacifist and homosexual who has found happiness in establishing and running the nursery with a partner called Gordon, a charismatic religious personality. David's most complete exposition of his views is offered to Mrs. Paget, the mother of Gordon, after her son's funeral:

> I think that passivity—I do not say quietism because that has religious connotations—is an entire way of living. . . . I'm not saying that the passive way of living is an absolute good, right at all times of history. . . . Only in ages like the present one, where violence and self-expression and complications of motive have become so great that we need to détente. . . . We need a simmering down of human personality, of human achievement too if you like, in order that we can start up again. Otherwise all will be lost in the boiling over. (290)

When Gordon dies, David is as lonely as his sister. At Andreadaswood, though, David believes "their fight for disciplined living" (133) has produced an inner peace. He is an intellectual who has left university life for a community which is a deliberate withdrawal from the world, though it is also commercially successful. The large house at the centre is the necessary setting that had given "enough room for privacy and communal living, for the quartet and writing their book." (142) It has been a life of work and high culture:

> For Gordon and himself, running the nursery had been the sealing of a bond of their life together . . . dilettante interests, an external pattern for their inner lives without which they might have succumbed to a corrosive anarchic existence. Yet it was always and however pleasantly a discipline, a renunciation of over indulgence in music or in books, or even, as Gordon admitted for himself of an exaggerated selfish engrossment in the life of the spirit. (148)

As David thinks over the life he has known with Gordon, he feels that it has given him strength to cope with the crises. But, in fact, Gordon's suffering causes him an intense anger which makes him write violently and in pain to Meg:

> God forgive me for prating about humanism, pretending that pain and evil could be reduced to a pigmy human stature. He equally fiercely attacked the monstrous Christianity that forbade Gordon the right to suicide and the wicked ideas of a good God and His gift of an Immortal soul that added the humiliation of a patience to Gordon's suffering. (240)

David's carefully evolved "stoic dignity" (241) cannot resolve the problem of human suffering. David writes immediately after this letter to excuse its stupidity, but it suggests the depths of the feelings which he usually and deliberately controls.

David's conscious philosophy is expressed fully in a conversation with Gordon's mother after the funeral. David is aware of the difficulty of not sounding pompous and academic but attaches so much importance to the ideas that he takes the risk of communication:

> I think it might be best to begin . . . by saying that if there's one word widely used today which I really abhor for its evasion and its looseness, that word is humanist. But the word has acquired by constant use of compendium significance combining a number of rather ill-linked views about life which, if only by their rather negative nature, it seems sensible to apply to me. I must accept. I'm afraid, being called a humanist. . . . Gordon as you know influenced me deeply, as he did everyone whom he met. I suppose I've had to fuse his way of life with my agnosticism. But I remain unconvinced by any transcendental arguments or, even more important, by any transcendental experiences that have been described to me. (289-90)

David's humanism has been influenced by the religious tradition of quietism. And it takes the form of which he calls "passivity" the reduction of human life from frenzied activity and from ideas of greatness, a "simmering down" to a safety point. (290)

The last part of the book describes the life of David and the convalescent Meg at Andreadaswood. Brother and sister come together for each other's consolation. Their evenings together become, in Meg's words, "a loving exchange of family snapshots." (343) For a while, Meg, prompted by interfering well-wishers whose psychology Wilson brilliantly exposes, works as secretary to a local headmaster. But she soon returns to her life with David, who feels pleased that he has helped her to develop an "inner strength." And they had both known "absolute despair and had not allowed it to turn to hatred." (392) One strange event mars the tranquil process. Meg insists on their giving a pre-Christmas party, and then behaves badly quite 'without her usual social deftness.' She talks all the time with an ambitious right wing M.P. called Michael Grant-Richards. David can excuse this by thinking that Grant-Richards had recalled Meg's dead husband. After this, Meg comes even closer to David, suggesting that he should abandon his work on a book about African flowers in a series begun with Gordon. And she wants his help in completing a book about the English novel. They begin to work with great pleasure. Indeed, one evening they have together in summer, talking about Godwin, seems to David "the happiest evening of his life." (420)

But this is not Meg Eliot's view. The following morning she makes suddenly the announcement that David has been expecting and fearing: she is to leave at once. She gives her reasons cogently:

> All this self-denial and self-discipline which seemed futile to me was what made you apart, withdrawn—what gave you that calm that saved me when I was lost. And now slowly but surely the calm is turning into plain self-indulgent apathy, the irksome discipline into pleasing triviality. And you just don't notice it, David, that's what I cannot understand. I have tried not to, but the sentimental, cosy futility of last night decided me. (425-26)

Meg must go, both for David's sake, since his strength comes from his loneliness, and for her own, for she cannot live fully outside ordinary society. This is what Grant-Richards has meant for her: "For me the only sense is to assert one's faith in people by living among them." (426) This she is beginning to do at the end of the novel, which ends with David: "David was always aware in the back of his mind he knew she would return; and being so aware, he ceased to feel the possibility as a very real one." (430) The reassurance is valuable to him, but what is emphasised is that human beings must accept responsibility for their own lives, and can, in doing so, hope to achieve a measure of fulfilment

This is linked to an insistence on the use of the human judgement which is common to brother and sister. David is disappointed by evidence of pettiness in Gordon just before his death. And he is tempted to say that he observes without judging:

> But the sentimentalism, that passed as a wide and deep love of humanity, as the gentle wisdom taught by the years, was surely the negation of real respect for men. It would never do, least of all when respect and love were involved. Where you respected and loved, you esteemed, you judged. (204)

Similarly, when Meg is trying to make a new life, she is told by her old friend Polly to follow her example of living on her capital and her wits. "And then you know lots of people to borrow from. That's what I've always done." (270) Meg finds, slightly to her own surprise, that she resents the advice: "you just have to settle for being a slut that's all." (272) She does not want an irresponsible Bohemian existence:

> Puritan or not, she was made differently—made to judge: and at this critical juncture she must make judgements or cease to exist. The truth was that Polly could be happy as she liked, her life was still a sort of animated death. . . . 'Loving the woman, yet hating her life.' Meg mocked at the conclusion she had reached. It was surely the most priggish

> of standpoints. Yet priggish or not, she knew that she must hold it. She was not looking for punchdrunk bliss or any other sort of plucky death in life. (273)

This sense of the interrelation of judgement, responsibility and selfhood is at the centre of Wilson's humanism. *The Middle Age of Mrs. Eliot* is successful in conveying through Meg Eliot and David Parker two forms of "humanistic"[17] achievement, active and passive responses to the challenges of modern life.

Speaking of his personal experiences, Angus Wilson recognizes that in *Hemlock and After* and again in *The Middle Age of Mrs. Eliot* he is trying to resolve a conflict between his "own liberal and humane attitude towards life and certain deep-seated, cruel instincts."[18]

III

Angus Wilson has done himself less than justice when he comments on the most striking incident in the novel where the relation between man and animal assumes an apparently predatory character. Wilson dwells for a long time on the events that occur at the cottage in Essex after Simon's escape from London. He stresses the fact that the journey was undertaken to preserve specimen animals for anatomical research is far removed from Simon's "considered reverence for animal life."[19]

Simon Carter behaves properly with a correct understanding of the relationship between men and animals, and he takes the decision to feed badgers. Here there is no sense of sadism and enjoyment. His later rejection of what he has done here is a perfectly natural response. It was horrible. But it was not enjoyable horrible. That is the difference between Bernard Sands (*Hemlock and After*) and Simon Carter. Near the beginning of *Hemlock and After*, Isabel Sands reflects on Bernard Sands's novel and finds them wanting: "she didn't care for her brothers' works, the earlier satirical ones seeming hard and frivolous—she felt they didn't do justice to the depth and courage of his humanity."[20]

In *The Old Men at the Zoo*, Angus Wilson describes the administration of a Zoo. He has attempted to place the London Zoo, with all its comic implications, against the background of an atomic war. His air evidently is to demonstrate that decisions for immediate survival must be made despite potential destruction. As in Snow's novels, man appears in his setting as a creature who has a duty to perform no matter what the circumstances, even the dubious job of evacuating Zoo animals after an atomic attack.

"Limited liberty"[21] is a phrase that might be used by Dr. Leacock, one of the old men in *The Old Men at Zoo*. It can mean very different things to different people, depending upon the view they take about what constitute the proper limits of personal satisfaction.

Leacock's intention in setting up his wildlife reserve is explained most fully in a television broadcast. He makes it when the project is still only a pious hope. In it he says that those "who profit by the naturalist way of life will be the pioneers in our society carrying the developed instinctual way of life to balance the top heavy intellectual growth of today."[22] He further says: after all because we do not want to live in chaos . . . there is no reason why in our fear we should die in captivity . . . liberty we can find if we accept some limitation on its definition, liberty thus limited we may feed on . . . only so I believe, can we restore the psychic balance, the soul's health of a very sick civilization."

In *The Old Men at Zoo*, Wilson explores the questions of personal versus public responsibility. He adopts the form of the novel as if it sets slightly in the course of future since his real interest is not in external trappings, but in perennial human problems. By taking the London Zoo and its four successive administrators as his central focus, Wilson contrasts the instinctual and rational motivations of human behaviour. He suggests how a proper human response should involve both. The Directors of the Zoo are so governed by some pet project which is a product of their particular monomanias. They eventually become incapable of responding adequately or at all to the other demands made upon them as director, husband, father or friend.

Simon Carter, the narrator of the event, is the Zoo's young Administrative Secretary. Relating to his personality, Sanderson has expressed his feelings in the following way:

> He looked down to where his toes must have been just visible to him beyond his little potbelly.
>
> He said solemnly, what was that chap's name, Carter, who declared that God was dead? To check my desire to laugh and to ward off Sanderson's intimacy, I [Simon Carter] could found only a vigorously facetious note.
>
> 'Nietzsche,' I replied, but you have to remember that he died off his nut.' It did not avail. In a way that makes it all the more moving, doesn't it? I wish I had more time for general culture. Things like today's damnable accident make one feel that he was right. Not believing in God, I can't pay much attention to rumours of his death. This more brutual line of defence proved equally unavailing, Sanderson looked up with a sort of shy reverence.
>
> 'I have always wanted to tell you, Carter, how much I admire the deeply felt quality of your agnosticism.' (20)

While the Director at the outset of their regimes appear pretty far gone in their monomania, the deterioration of Carter is gradual. At the start he is potentially a responsive human being. He identifies himself ever more closely with an ideal of administrative responsibility. By the end of the novel his promising responsiveness is completely lost. He qualifies for a Directorship himself and begins actively campaigning for the job. Simon Carter explains his view of life in the following way:

> For a few seconds the sharp terror tightened my breathing and constricted my scrotum. But it had happened now so often and so pointlessly that it quickly vanished into the sea of anxious doubts in which like everyone else I had learned to swim my life. It was followed by a more selfless yet no less genuine sorrow for the obliteration of human crea-

> tion—conventional thoughts of human struggle and human hope and human happiness gave me for a moment a no less conventional choke in my throat. Yet this also was too customary a sadness to last for more than a minute or two. To such quickly effected emotions had years of war alarms brought so many of us. In the end I could only really feel anxious as to how Martha would take this latest scare. As if, from previous experience I didn't know. (64)

In many ways the opening episode of the book becomes a central focus for subsequent events. Derek Filson, a young keeper, is killed by a sick giraffe. But surpassing the horror of the accident is the response to it from almost every quarter. Dr. Leacock, the Director of the Zoo, views the incident as a possible asset in the scheme for National Reserve outside London to replace Regent's Park. The novelist is writing about the views of Dr. Leacock in this way: "Of course, Leacock told us, this doesn't mean that the intellectual workers with all that they have done and will do for humanity do not still have a central place in Zoological studies." (122)

Sir Robert Falcon, Curator of Mammals and once Britain's most famous explorer, becomes a scapegoat for the affair. He neither reprimands his chief keeper nor sees to it that appropriate precautions are taken in the future. Even the boy's parents fail to respond with proper concern for what has happened. Mr. Falcon is anxious to avoid scandal with his wife and wishes for still other reasons simply to let matters rest. Simon Carter expresses his feelings of the death of Filson in this way:

> "Unfortunately a young keeper was left to look after the animal and lost his life as a result. He looked surprised. That really isn't anything to do with me. That was Falcon's affair. Of course, you may well feel that you have to criticise him, since it's a matter of use of staff, but . . ."
>
> I asked "isn't it a question of humanity?"

"Humanity would be all right if things were run properly. This young keeper's death is a very good example of that." (144)

In the midst of all this expediency and evasion, Simon Carter tries to launch an investigation. He believes that he is moved by a sincere regard for human life. It is based more upon the concrete reality of young Filson's suffering than upon his own slight acquaintance with the boy. He does not recognize that his concern is partly an abstraction of his self-righteous conscience or priggishness. Carter's dwindling capacity for human relationships and his final revulsion from them are reflected in his experiences with all the Directors under whom he works, but primarily with Dr. Leacock. He expressed his views to Dr. Leacock, thus:

> No, no, Sir. He knew nothing of it then. No, it was strawson. It was the first he had realized of my determination. He came out strong against me as I said. No knowledge of mammals, rare and costly beast, criticism of his management, slip that wouldn't happen again—I had the lot of it. But I wasn't going to budge. He begged me for the animal, Sir. He bred it himself, Sir, at Regent's Park. And from what he'd always said they aren't easy to breed in captivity. But I simply said to him, "you aren't taking risks with human life again." . . . What I hadn't reckoned with was his going to Lord Godmanchester. And before I could say another thing Lord Godmanchester cancelled my orders. I was very angry, Sir, I must tell you. And I had words with him. I dare say that he did more harm than good. (203)

Under Leacock's plan for a National Reserve, animals may enjoy the fine compromise of 'Limited Liberty.' Simon Carter serves jointly as Warden of native British Wildlife and as Administrative Secretary for the whole park. In this way, he hopes to reconcile pleasures with duty and so ends the "bifurcation of his life." (156-57)

As work on the Reserve begins, Leacock and his wife move from London to take charge. Harriet, his daughter is legally restricted to their supervision because of the latest in her series of misdemeanours like the animals. She is also to enjoy only 'Limited Liberty'. It is during this period that Simon Carter, who has brought himself to the project, first encounters Harriet's demands upon him. It is her sexual demands that he is unable to satisfy. He cannot make the kind of response that would provide a human focus for her and so temper the animalism to which she is being driven for satisfying relationship. Under her present confinement, without the prospect of some rewarding human intercourse, she turns in despair to her pet mastiff which kills her.

The manner of Harriet's death gives Godmanchester all he needs to relax her father's hold on the Reserve. In this situation Carter can force the weapon out of Godmanchester's hands boldly proclaiming what really has happened. Leacock makes him consider the possible effect of the truth upon his wife. She believes her daughter has been killed by another escaped animal. Such confrontation is based upon meeting Mrs. Leacock in a way that her husband refuses to do as a person. It proves too much for Carter and he again backs away from that responsibility. The physical violence had done to the possibility of human dialogue and to human dignity.

These episodes suggest further deterioration in the life of Simon Carter. His wife Martha explains her relationship with other person to him in this manner:

> She said, "Anyway your old formula—No sex without real affection—wouldn't have kept me on the straight and narrow path. I truly am very fond of Bobby. I must tell you. I went today to the hospital to ask, about him. He has been allowed to go home. Oh don't worry. I shan't go near him again. I've done enough harm. But I am very fond of him, and I was very, very sorry for him."
>
> "But you can't mix up being sorry with sexul love."

> "Can't I darling? I've told you I am a very confused person. Awfully maternal anyway. I think I'm always very ready to be protecting someone I love. And when I feel protecting I want him to take me to bed if it gives him pleasure. I think that's the basis of all sex for me really. Oh, I don't know." (284)

The breakdown of responsibility in the sphere of individual human relations corresponds to a similar breakdown in the administrative responsibility for the Zoo. In the end it almost turns into a Roman Circus—and ultimately the failure of civilized nations rises above a politics of power upheld by the use of nuclear weapons.

Simon Carter in the administration of Wilson's Zoo adopts himself to one directorship after another until, like Gulliver, he loses all sense of the necessary balance in human nature. He helps other people at the risk of his own life. The novelist describes it in the following manner:

> Before I [Carter] could answer, Beard had leapt from the Lorry and was standing before them with a revolver in his hand. I shall shoot any one who comes near—his voice sounded higher than usual but even more prim. I called, "Really Beard. Don't be ridiculous." . . . As she was talking I saw that her son and one of the older men had begun to move out of the circle. . . . I flung myself upon him and we fell hard on to the ground. His revolver flew from his hand, scudding across the ground to come to rest at the old woman's feet. She picked it up and came towards us. For a moment I thought that she hit Beard sharply across the side of his hand with her stick . . . such a lot of people lose control at a time like this. Poor man." (301-2)

Under the Zoo's fourth and most notorious Director, he begins to yearn for a life based solely upon rational controls epitomised by Englander's policy of "competence, good sense and above all moderation" (321) and to covet the power that such rationalism affords.

The Old Men at the Zoo inverts the pattern of Wilson's previous novels and gives full vent to his satiric impulse. Like the other heroes, Simon Carter has at first a remarkable gift of irony, including self-irony which makes him an excellent agent of satire. But in the unfolding of events, he steadily changes like Gulliver from the instrument of satire to its object. Instead of becoming aware like Bernard Sands or Meg Eliot, of his delusions and self-deceptions, he falls more and more their victim, rejecting whatever help is offered to him by his wife and others.

In the discussion of *The Middle Age of Mrs. Eliot* and *The Old Men at the Zoo* we find that the sense of love and sympathetic attitude towards human beings as well as animals may be considered some of the constituents of the humanism of Angus Wilson.

Meg Eliot, the protagonist of *The Middle Age of Mrs. Eliot* comes in contact with the hard and bare truths of life when her husband dies leaving her childless and without sufficient resources to support herself. Many people try to give her solace but she gets peace only after she comes to her brother David who is a man of helping attitude. David leaves his university education to involve himself into the activities of the welfare of his community. He helps Gordon very much and becomes very miserable when the latter dies. When his sister Meg Eliot comes to him, he helps her beyond his capacity. It is only due to the encouragement of David that Meg becomes bold to lead her life.

Similarly, Simon Carter (*The Old Men at the Zoo*) is very helpful. He has love for human beings as well as for the animals. Therefore when he is appointed the Administrative Secretary of the London Zoo, he becomes very happy and hopes to reconcile his pleasure with duty to serve the animals from the core of his heart.

NOTES

1. E.M. Forster, *Two Cheers for Democracy* (London: Penguin), p. 64.

2. George Wickers, *Masters of the Modern British Fiction* (New York: Macmillan, 1963), p. 387.
3. J.L. Halio, *Angus Wilson* (Edinburgh and London: Oliver & Boyd, 1964), p. 27.
4. K.W. Grandson, "Angus Wilson," Ian Scott Kilvert, ed., *Writers and Their Works,* No. 208 (London: Longman Green, 1969), p. 9.
5. *Ibid.*, p.17.
6. Jim Hunter, ed., *The Modern Novel in English* (London: Faber and Faber, 1966), p. 164.
7. Bernard Bergonzi, "Angus Wilson," D.L. Kirkpatrick, ed., *Contemporary Novelists,* p. 809.
8. *Loc. cit.*
9. Angus Wilson, *The Middle Age of Mrs. Eliot* (London: Secker & Warburg, 1980), p. 1.
10. *Loc. cit.*
11. L.P. Hartley, *The Novelist's Responsibility* (Great Britain: Hamilton, 1967), p. 190.
12. Colin Wilson, *The Age of Defeat* (London: Victor Gollancz, 1954), p. 69.
13. E.M. Forster, *Howards End* (London: Edward Arnold, 1910), p. 171.
14. V.A. Shahane, *E.M. Forster: A Resentment* (Bombay: Kitab Mahal, 1962), p. 96.
15. Herbert Read, *English Prose Style* (Bell, 1928), p. 136.
16. Bernard Bergonzi, p.890.
17. David Daiches, *The Penguin Companion to Literature Britain and Commonwealth* (London: The Penguin Press, 1971), p. 557.
18. *Twentieth Century Literature,* p. 97.
19. Patrick Swiden, *The English Novel of History and Society* (London: Macmillan, 1984), p. 168.
20. *Ibid.*
21. James Gindin, *Post-War British Fiction: New Accents and Attitudes,* p. 1962.
22. Angus Wilson, *The Old Man at Zoo* (London: Panther Granada, 1979), p. 118.

Chapter VIII

CONCLUSION

It is often said that the novel is a dying art. Arnold Kettle has also described "narrowness and pessimism"[1] as the two characteristics of the contemporary novel. But Angus Wilson is of the view that the novel is not a dying art, it will remain alive till human beings exist on the earth because he considers human beings as the nourishment of the novelists. He further says: "As small dinosaurs lived upon certain vegetable materials and the great dinosaurs lived upon the small dinosaurs . . . the vegetable matter withered away and the small dinosaurs found nothing to feed upon and they died away, and the great dinosaurs also disappeared because they had nothing to eat . . . and perhaps if the novelist does disappear."[2]

In the past his society supplied the artist with both values and symbols that passed current everywhere. Today, however, the responsible artist stands alone in a shifting world with the winds of a hundred doctrines howling about him, where there was one solemn mystery, there are now manifold vexing riddles. Where the older writers saw an order whose larger purposes were responsible or even benevolent, the modern writer can see only a 'meaningless welter' and 'immense indifference' in the absence of a firmly established school to nurture him. This is not only true to the artist and older writers but is equally true in every respect to the novelists. It is meaningful in this context to quote the words of Walter Allen: "Every novelist, then gives us in his novels his own personal idiosyncratic vision of the world. The vision is acted out by images of men and women. It is, so to speak, populated; and this is why we may quite legitimately talk about a novelist's 'world.' We mean by it the whole realm of his imagination as he has put it down on paper and we mean further that this realm, fictitious though it is, is yet somehow a self-contained entity consistent in itself and conforming to the psychological laws which govern its creator and his response to life. To create such a world is not the highest achievement of a novelist, but unless he does so he will never reach the highest."[3]

The novelists also find themselves lonely in the modern strife-torn world, like the artist and other writers who are fighting for achieving solution of the problems and sufferings of human beings. Similarly their protagonists, too, find themselves alone in the hostile world. They truly represent their creators and they do not leave any stone unturned in solving the problems and sufferings of human beings. Sometimes they revolt against the norms and the condition of society and sometimes they grudge against the filthy rich who are responsible for creating artificial circumstances to trap the downtrodden in their nets. Today some novelists namely Angus Wilson, William Golding, John Wain, Kingsley Amis, Iris Murdoch and Doris Lessing involve in finding possible solution of the problems and sufferings of human beings. They possess the humanistic traits in themselves for the benefit of the underdogs.

First of all we may cite the example of Angus Wilson. He is always concerned with what he has discovered about human emotions. All morals are in a sense steps to self-realization to him. "Despite the moral and metaphysical pre-occupation" which Wilson says, "a serious novelist must have,"[4] he feels that any dogmatic or prophetic approach by the writer ultimately proves destructive to his art. His characters, generally, retain an immediacy towards life, not a set of rules applied to life in advance.

Angus Wilson is of the view that the English novel stands today around a humanistic concept of the world which is deeply human-centred. He regards man as the essential centre of the world. He like E.M. Forster believes that the individual "human norm is the measure of everything."[5] A similar view is also expressed by Dr. Shankar, the protagonist of Mulk Raj Anand's novel *The Private Life of an Indian Prince* (1953). Dr. Shankar believes in man rather than god: "he is the final fact of the universe. There is nothing higher and more dignified than human existence."[6] A little further he expresses his disbelief in any supernatural fate or transcendental reality and his faith that man is his own sanction. He says: "I don't believe that there is any power transcending man who can decide things for him."[7]

Angus Wilson is regarded as the darling of the intellectuals. He digs deep into the roots of human morality and comes up with good and evil. Meg Eliot, the protagonist of *The Middle Age of Mrs. Eliot,* tries to lead her life sensibly and to do good for others. In her life generally she is drawn to people and she is compassionate towards them. But, of course, her life is founded on a hollow basis, as she is to discover when she learns her husband dies a bankrupt as a result of his compulsive gambling. After the death of her husband, she faces the miseries of her life boldly and later gets stability in life.

David ignores the active role. However he realises contemplation as a great necessity in the world. Meg, in the early part of her life has failed to contemplate at all. David has learned the need for contemplation, but unfortunately he contemplates only and is incapable of action.

The Old Men at the Zoo is set for its central character Simon Carter. He has the sense of love not only for mankind but for animals as well. Therefore, in providing proper care to the animals in the London Zoo, he is humiliated several times by the Directors of the Zoo. According to Angus Wilson, Golding is not a humanist. He says: "William Golding is the nearest to any of us writing in England who is not a humanist."[8] But in the defence of the charge, William Golding owns that he is a religious novelist and believes that some people are saints in *Lord of the Files*. Simon is a saint; that is why he says that literary people have found Simon incomprehensible but he is comprehensible to the illiterate person. They believe in saints and sanctity. William Golding believes in human guilt and the human sense of paradise lost. He believes in divine mercy also. Thus he is very close to

Alexander Pope when the latter says 'to err is human, to forgive is divine.'

Golding's second novel, *The Inheritors*, is the story of accumulation of guilt that necessarily attended the historical success of Homo sapiens; the intellectual superiority of Man over his simian victims is precisely measured by the cruelty and guilt which dominate his life.

Of all the novels of William Golding, *Lord of the Flies* and *The Inheritors* are the most successful; they deal with humanity and evil. They present a general and panoramic view of life. In both the novels, human malevolence manifests itself in the arena of power, most fearsomely through mob atrocity. Thus it is seen that evil is something inherent in man in the fictional universe of William Golding.

The most notorious literary revolt of the so-called "Angry Young Men" of the fifties is associated with the names of John Wain, Kingsley Amis and John Osborne. The first thing to note about them is certain bluntness in their language and down-to-earth quality in their attitudes. John Wain, one of the important members of the group, first becomes widely known as a humorist and iconoclast. His first novel *Hurry on Down* became a symbol for the irreverent rootlessness of the younger generation. The protagonist of the novel Charles Lumley comes from the middle class and he always devotes himself in doing well for the people of his class. Wain's perspective is that of the man of orthodox common sense, the defender of a basic human dignity against the absurd pretences of the modern world. Even the figure of despair, the central character, Edgar Banks of *Living in the Present*, about to commit suicide, decides that he cannot do so unless he also rids the world of the most loathsome and amoral creatures he knows.

Unlike John Wain, Kingsley Amis is not an iconoclast. In his first novel *Lucky Jim* the protagonist Jim Dixon is helped materially by an aristocrat, a symbolic representative of the pinnacle of society who leans down like a fairy god-father to reward the deserving. At the end of the novel, Jim Dixon, less arid and phoney as a teacher than are the other academics is rewarded because "it's not that you've got the qualifications, though and that's much rarer."[9]

The revolt of Jim Dixon is not a revolt against anything that can be described as academic values liberal or otherwise. His level of revolt is Amis's level of revolt. Therefore, Jim Dixon is regarded as the mouthpiece for the expression of Amis's own dissatisfaction and annoyance with the world.

In *That Uncertain Feeling*, the protagonist, John Lewis is always aware of his dignity but sometimes he detracts from the path and becomes the pawn and plays in the hands of rich people. But very soon he realizes and becomes able to save his married life as well as his dignity after settling down in his native town Fforestfawr.

On the other hand, the fiction of Iris Murdoch suggests the range of human thought, the classically philosophical as well as the linguistic and ethical. 'The novels like *The Sandcastle* and *The Bell* are elaborate constructions of human identity and are presented with striking drama in metaphors like scaling towers and dredging sunken bells from lakes in which the creature is visible despite the impossibility of his or her project.

Bradley Pearson, the main character of *The Black Prince*, always has the sense of sympathetic and helping attitude to the members of the family of his rival novelist Arnold Baffin. He realizes his duties of a brother to help his ailing sister and as an artist to write his magnum opus.

In the novels of Iris Murdoch, the human being is tested by his response to or possible recovery from pain and deprivation. The forms of response are various and imaginative. Yet, in her world, despite all the pain of existence, most people resist the safety and stasis of the enclosures of the incompletely knowable self.

Doris Lessing's fierce reformist spirit pervades her writings; her anger and indignation at society's mishandling of its concerns is still very much with her. Her disillusionment is tempered by wisdom learned through living.

Her writings extend the boundaries of fictional experiment with different genres, explore the world of Africa, Britain and other places and offer a socio-political and cultural commentary of the post modern world. She is descendent of those nineteenth century women writers who made "poverty class-conflict, Women's suffrage and slavery the subjects of their novels."[10] It is rightly said that Lessing is deeply concerned with the human condition.

The Golden Notebook is greeted as her feminist manifesto. It is as much a book about writing as it is an exploration of women's relationships with each other and man. The novel consists of largely of the notebooks which the central character Anna Wulf keeps. It is impressive in its honesty, integrity and unique as an exposition of the emotional problems that face an intelligent woman who wants to live in the kind of freedom a man may take for granted.

In *The Four-Gated City*, Martha's most vital sexual experiences are with men who are flawed prophets. Thomas cannot pass beyond violence and chaos; Jack transmogrifies his knowledge of the body into sadistic domination; Mark cannot transcend rationalism despite his brains, strength and kindness.

Thus it may be seen that the mood and motive behind the writing of these novelists clearly shows that all of them are humanists in their own way. For example, Angus Wilson and William Golding oppose each other—the former is an agnostic humanist but the latter is a religious humanist. Angus Wilson has no faith in any source of values beyond this world but William Golding does have faith in such sources of values. Golding believes that supernatural help may solve the problems of human beings and it also gives them courage to face boldly the miseries of life. In Angus Wilson we find the sense of love and sympathetic attitude towards human beings as well as animals, which shows the humanistic qualities while in William Golding we find the Christian traits like original sin, sense of evil and guilt as the constituents of his humanism

John Wain and Kingsley Amis belong to 'Angry Young Men' group of novelists. Therefore, they revolt against the prevailing norms and conditions of the society. On the one hand they have the sense of helping attitude towards their fellow beings that generally belong to lower middle class, and on the other hand they are very critical of the filthy rich whose solitary aim is to acquire wealth by any means. Basically, they are the champions who preserve the human values and dignity.

So far as Iris Murdoch and Doris Lessing are concerned, the former believes in the realization of guilt, repentance and love as the sublimation of humanity while Doris Lessing is devoted to the cause of women and the 'blacks.' She is very anxious to uplift the condition of women in men's society and the status of the 'blacks' in Africa.

Although these novelists share no group moral position as they share no specific political doctrine, they occupy themselves with moral and human issues that are specifically social and political.

The humanist's faith rests not on an explanation but on experience of value in the human tradition. It also rests in individual relationship between man and nature, man and man and man and woman. All these things are answer enough to the goodness of life and to the creative energies of man's spirit.

NOTES

1. Arnold Kettle, *An Introduction to English Novel*, p. 166.
2. Angus Wilson, "Dilemma of the Contemporary Novelist," *Diversity and Depth in Fiction*, ed. Karry Mcsweeney, p. 238.
3. Walter Allen, *The English Novel* (Harmondsworth: Penguin, 1954), p. 17.
4. J.L. Halio, *Angus Wilson*, p. 101.
5. Fredrick C. Crews, *The Perils of Humanism*, p. 6.
6. G.S. Balarama Gupta, *Mulk Raj Anand* (Bareilly: Prakash, 1974), p. 85.
7. *Ibid.*, p. 85.
8. Angus Wilson, "Dilemma of the Contemporary Novelist," p. 247.
9. Kingsley Amis, *Lucky Jim*, p. 140.
10. Carol Simpson Stern, "Doris Lessing," *Contemporary Novelists*, ed. D.L. Kirkpatrick, p. 531.